A Deacon's Guide to Baptizing Children

A Pastoral and Theological Approach

Paul F. Covino

LITURGY
TRAINING
PUBLICATIONS

Nihil Obstat
Rev. Mr. Daniel G. Welter, JD
Chancellor
Archdiocese of Chicago
August 2, 2021

Imprimatur
Very Rev. Robert G. Casey
Vicar General
Archdiocese of Chicago
August 2, 2021

The *Nihil Obstat* and *Imprimatur* are declarations that the material is free from doctrinal or moral error, and thus is granted permission to publish in accordance with c. 827. No legal responsibility is assumed by the grant of this permission. No implication is contained herein that those who have granted the *Nihil Obstat* and *Imprimatur* agree with the content, opinions, or statements expressed.

This book was edited by Mary G. Fox. Michael A. Dodd was the production editor, Juan Alberto Castillo was the designer, and Kari Nicholls was the production artist.

Cover photo by © John Zich.

Photos on pages 1, 67 © LTP; pages 25, 29, 32, 54, 73 © John Zich; page 49 by Karen Ramos.

26 25 24 23 22   1 2 3 4 5

Printed in the United States of America

Library of Congress Control Number: 2021939758

ISBN: 978-1-61671-600-4

DBC

Contents

Part 3
Nurturing Faith in Families

PART 1

Reflecting on the Gift of Baptism

Chapter 1

The Call of Baptism

A colleague with years of experience as a retreat director once warned, "If you aren't prepared to hear God tell you to do something different, then don't go on a retreat!" Those words echoed in my mind during a five-day silent retreat several years ago as I wrestled with thoughts that had been recurring over the previous few years. I was not experiencing what Ignatian spirituality refers to as *desolation* but rather a sense of *stagnation* in my work. For thirty years, I had been privileged to labor at something that I truly loved: Catholic liturgy. I had taught, led workshops, directed conferences, authored articles and a book, and served as liturgy director for two parishes, a graduate ministry program, and a Catholic college. In my younger years, I had considered priesthood but discerned that marriage was my true vocation, and I had happily served as a lay ecclesial minister with a wonderful wife and four sons. I still enjoyed my work and many great relationships with ordained, religious, and lay colleagues in ministry, but I was feeling stagnant professionally. As I prayed about this "stirring of my soul" during the retreat, two ideas emerged as a way to proceed: pursue a leadership position in campus ministry and explore ordination as a deacon. My colleague was right: God had indeed used the retreat to tell me to do something different.

A few years later, as a fellow deacon vested me with the stole and dalmatic during the ordination liturgy, an important truth became very clear: just as the stole and dalmatic were placed on top of my alb, so my ordination as a deacon was another way in which God was calling me to answer the call of my baptism. It was the next step in a journey that had begun decades earlier when my parents presented me for baptism, wearing a white baptismal garment. Reminders of that baptismal garment reappeared in the crisp white shirt I wore for my first Communion, the robe I wore for my confirmation, the formal white shirt I wore for my wedding, the alb I wore as a lay minister at various liturgies, and the alb that served as the foundation for the stole and dalmatic at my ordination. One day, that baptismal garment will reappear in the form of the pall that will cover the casket at my funeral. The baptismal garment is the common thread that connects the milestones in my response to the call of my baptism.

In between these milestones have been times of formation and various other opportunities to answer the call of my baptism, that is, to "share in the common priesthood of all believers"[1] and to "embrace the lifelong journey of discipleship."[2] While these terms were not common among Catholics when I was growing up, I nevertheless saw in the example of my parents that being a member of the Church involved participating in Sunday Mass, serving in parish ministries, and responding to the needs of the poor. Mentors in high school and college helped me to see and experience the Church as the People of God[3] and the Body of Christ,[4] and they shared their passion for faith and particularly for Catholic liturgy with me. With their encouragement and the supportive advice of my parents, I took the first major leap of faith in my life and shifted my course of studies from premed to theology with a focus on liturgy. While I was not familiar with the term "vocational discernment" at the time, I realized in retrospect that this leap of faith was my way of leaning into my vocation, described by Frederick Buechner as "the work a man is called to by God . . . [that is] the place where your deep gladness and the world's deep hunger meet."[5]

As a husband and father, marriage and family life have been privileged places to answer the call of my baptism. I have experienced in the love of my wife "an image of the absolute and unfailing love with which God loves man,"[6] and marriage challenges me each day "to overcome self-absorption, egoism, pursuit of [my] own pleasure, and to open [myself] to the other, to mutual aid and to self-giving."[7]

---

1. *Catechism of the Catholic Church* (CCC), 1268.
2. Mary A. Ehle, *Baptized for Discipleship: The Meaning of Baptism for Our Christian Life* (Chicago: Liturgy Training Publications [LTP], 2019), 2.
3. *Lumen gentium* (LG), 9, 31.
4. 1 Corinthians 12:27.
5. Frederick Buechner, *Wishful Thinking: A Theological ABC* (New York: Harper and Row, 1973), 95.
6. CCC, 1604.
7. CCC, 1609.

Our marriage has matured "in good times and in bad, in sickness and in health"[8] as we have learned to celebrate and thank God for blessings and graces and to support each other and seek God's help through challenges and times of desolation. We have welcomed four sons "lovingly from God and [sought] to bring them up according to the law of Christ and his Church,"[9] and we have trusted in God's abiding presence through a miscarriage and a car accident that left our oldest son with a traumatic brain injury. As we have celebrated the baptisms of grandchildren and the funeral liturgies of parents, we have seen the words of the psalmist come to life: "One generation shall laud your works to another, / and shall declare your mighty acts."[10]

An unexpected invitation from a colleague to serve in college campus ministry led to another way of answering the call of my baptism through the opportunity to "tell the next generation / that this is God, / our God forever and ever."[11] Over the course of almost three decades in campus ministry at two colleges in the same city,[12] I have been able to accompany undergraduate students as they have prayed and worshiped, wrestled with the implications of their faith, sought meaning in their joys and struggles, and tried to discern their vocation in life. Ministering with a wide variety of students, faculty, administrators, and staff has helped me to appreciate both the diversity present among the people of God's creation and the spiritual discipline that is required to sustain and nurture communion and unity among those who are Roman Catholics. I have been inspired, as well as challenged, by students who advocate passionately for the social teachings of the Church and even dedicate a postgraduate year to service among the needy in an organization such as the Jesuit Volunteer Corps and by students who are devoted to adoration of the Blessed Sacrament and even dedicate a postgraduate year to evangelization on a college campus in an organization such as the Fellowship of Catholic University Students. Participation in the Catholic Common Ground Initiative has reinforced my fundamental belief that "we were all baptized into one body"[13] and has shaped my approach to

---

8. *Order of Celebrating Matrimony* (OCM), 62.
9. OCM, 60.
10. Psalm 145:4.
11. Psalm 48:13–14.
12. College of the Holy Cross (1993–2014) and Assumption University (2014–present), both in Worcester, Massachusetts.
13. 1 Corinthians 12:13.

ministry based on "a common ground centered on faith in Jesus, marked by accountability to the living Catholic tradition, and ruled by a renewed spirit of civility, dialogue, generosity, and broad and serious consultation."[14] Having ministered first among members of Generation X (born 1965–1979), then Generation Y (born 1980–1994, also known as the millennials), and now Generation Z (born 1995–2015), I have also seen firsthand the downward trend in religious affiliation. As a campus minister, I have become increasingly convinced of the need to respond to my baptismal call to "go therefore and make disciples of all nations."[15]

Ministry as a deacon has provided other opportunities to answer the call of my baptism. Prominent among them is the ministry of proclaiming and preaching the Word of God. I am challenged regularly by the words that the bishop spoke to me as he placed the *Book of the Gospels* in my hands: "Receive the Gospel of Christ whose herald you have become. Believe what you read, teach what you believe, and practice what you teach."[16] As I prepare my homilies and then preach, I have to confront the extent to which my life does or does not reflect the Gospel I proclaim. I have come to appreciate the wisdom in one of the closing paragraphs of the preaching document from the bishops of the United States: "We too stand in sacred space, aware of our personal inadequacy, yet willing to share how the scriptural story has become integrated into our thoughts and actions while we walked among those who turn their faces toward us."[17] Similarly, as I speak with engaged couples in premarital meetings and with parents in prebaptismal meetings and as I preside and preach at the celebrations of matrimony and baptism, I am both renewed in and humbled by the vision of Christian spouses and Christian parents that these sacraments proclaim. My preaching and the formation that I seek to facilitate in the preparatory meetings invite these couples and parents to embrace this vision, but it also compels me to reflect on how adequately I am living out my vocation as a Christian husband and father.

Whether as an invitation to do something different while on a retreat or the daily reminders in my life as a member of the priesthood of believers, as a husband, as a father and grandfather, as a campus

---

14. Catholic Common Ground Initiative, *Called to Be Catholic: Church in a Time of Peril*.
15. Matthew 28:19.
16. *Rite of Ordination of Deacons*, 210.
17. National Conference of Catholic Bishops, *Fulfilled in Your Hearing: The Homily in the Sunday Assembly* (1982), 115.

minister, and as a deacon, God continuously offers me ways to answer the call of my baptism. To minister effectively and authentically to people who are preparing for and celebrating baptism, I need to be aware of this and able to articulate it with my voice and reflect it in my life. In other words, I need to be in touch with who I am as a disciple of Jesus Christ. Brother deacon, I trust that this book is in your hands because you also want to be as effective and authentic as possible in your ministry with those who are preparing for and celebrating baptism. So, before you turn to the next chapter of this book, I invite you to take some time to reflect on how baptism has shaped and continues to shape your life.

Reflection Questions

1. How have you answered the call of your baptism in your various roles: as a member of the priesthood of believers; as a colleague among your coworkers; as a son; as a husband, single man, or widower; as a father; as an uncle; as a grandfather; as a deacon?

2. Pope Francis has written that "being a disciple means being constantly ready to bring the love of Jesus to others, and this can happen unexpectedly and in any place: on the street, in a city square, during work, on a journey."[18] How does this affirm your response to your baptism, that is, your discipleship, and how does it challenge it?

---

18. Pope Francis, *Evangelii gaudium* (*The Joy of the Gospel*) [EG], 127.

Chapter 2

The Meaning of the Rite

Lex orandi, lex credendi was a common phrase that I learned when I studied liturgy in graduate school. It is an abbreviated form of a longer saying attributed to Prosper of Aquitaine in the fifth century, and it is translated and explained in the *Catechism of the Catholic Church*: "The law of prayer is the law of faith: the Church believes as she prays. Liturgy is a constitutive element of the holy and living Tradition."[1] Some liturgical theologians develop this principle and speak of the liturgy as the Church's "primary theology" or the Church's "faith in motion."[2] Pope Francis has referred to the liturgy as "the first 'teacher' of catechism."[3] Applied to baptism, this principle suggests that the celebration of baptism shapes and forms our understanding of baptism through its gestures, movements, symbols, and texts. This does not diminish the importance of resources such as the *Catechism of the Catholic Church*, but it reminds us that the most immediate way in which most people encounter the Church's understanding of baptism is through participation in the baptismal liturgy. As deacons who assist and preside at celebrations of baptism, we need to appreciate the meaning of this rite.

Procession: Our Journey to God

Catholic liturgies are not static; they involve movement. Think of the procession in which we deacons take the *Book of the Gospels* from the altar to the ambo, the procession of members of the assembly to receive the Body and Blood of Christ, the procession with palms at the beginning

---

1. CCC, 1124.

2. Aidan Kavanagh, *On Liturgical Theology* (Collegeville, MN: Liturgical Press, 1992), 8.

3. Address to Italian Association of Saint Cecilia, Rome, September 28, 2019, https://www.vaticannews.va /en/pope/news/2019-09/pope-francis-sacred-music-association-cecilia-audience.html.

of the Palm Sunday liturgy, the procession with the paschal candle at the beginning of the Easter Vigil, and the processions at the beginning and end of Mass. The baptismal liturgy unfolds at four stations in the church, and there are processions to and from each of them: the entrance of the church, the ambo, the baptismal font, and the altar. Each of these stations and processions reveals something about our journey to God.

The Entrance of the Church

As any parent knows, the very act of getting to church with children can be a major accomplishment. In baptism, this act begins with the parents' decision to seek baptism for their child. Between 2000 and 2018, the number of children baptized in the Catholic Church in the United States decreased by 38 percent.[4] Even if parents do not articulate this well, in seeking baptism for their child, they are making an increasingly counter-cultural response to a call from God to share their faith with their child. To follow through on this decision, they and their child will need "the community of believers. It is only within the faith of the Church that each of the faithful can believe."[5] As parents make the figurative procession from the moment they inquire about having their child baptized to the moment they arrive at the entrance of the church for the baptism, everything we do as deacons should manifest the Church's desire to support the parents in their response to a call from God.

This spirit of support continues in the baptismal liturgy, which begins at the entrance of the church where the parents and their child are welcomed and assured of the parish community's "support in raising your children / in the practice of the faith."[6] While it is the priest or deacon who extends this greeting and assurance to the parents, the *Order of Baptism of Children* assumes that other members of the local community are also present. Their presence reveals our conviction that the child to be baptized "has the right to the love and help of the community."[7] This is why the *Order of Baptism of Children* gives preference to celebrating baptism at the Easter Vigil or at a Sunday Mass "so that the whole community may be able to take part in the rite"[8] and so that "it becomes

---

4. Center for Applied Research in the Apostolate, "Frequently Requested Church Statistics," https://cara.georgetown.edu/frequently-requested-church-statistics/.

5. CCC, 1253.

6. *Order of Baptism of Children* (OBC), 36.

7. OBC, 4.

8. OBC, 9.

apparent that the faith in which the children are being baptized is a treasure not belonging to the family alone, but to the whole Church of Christ."[9] The presence and participation of other members of the Church beyond the family testifies to our belief that, through baptism, we "are incorporated into the Church and made sharers in her mission."[10] As baptism is considered "the door to life and to the Kingdom,"[11] the entrance of the church represents the door that Christ holds open to all, the door that opens onto our common pilgrimage through eternal life. This pilgrimage is made not alone but with members of the Body of Christ. While on occasion pastoral reasons may exist for celebrating a baptism with the participation of only the family, making this a regular practice leaves the promise of community support and a shared life in the Body of Christ sounding rather hollow.

The Ambo

From the entrance, the parents process with their child and the godparents into the church and take their place among the members of the worshiping assembly. There, the attention turns to the second station: the ambo where the Scriptures that "nourish and govern the whole Christian life"[12] are proclaimed. When the baptism of a child is celebrated, the ambo represents the role that the Scriptures play in the formation of the child being baptized, of the child's parents, and of the whole Christian community. While adult catechumens are formed through the Scriptures over a period of time prior to baptism, children who are baptized "cannot profess the faith for themselves"[13] and are formed in the faith over a period of time after baptism. Just as Scripture plays an integral role in the formation of adult catechumens, so Scripture plays an equally important role in the postbaptismal formation of children that is intended to "lead them little by little to discern God's plan in Christ, so that ultimately they may be able to ratify the faith in which they have been baptized."[14]

While the Scriptures will be part of the child's postbaptismal formation, the proclamation of Scripture at the baptismal liturgy is

9. OBC, 4.
10. CCC, 1213.
11. *Christian Initiation:* General Introduction (CI), 3.
12. CCC, 141.
13. OBC, 1.
14. OBC, 3.

primarily "intended to stir up the faith of the parents and godparents and others present."[15] The *Order of Baptism of Children* even suggests that "while the Liturgy of the Word is celebrated, it is desirable that children should be taken to a separate place. But care should be taken that the parents and godparents attend the Liturgy of the Word; the children should therefore be entrusted to the care of others."[16] As many of us know from experience, it can be difficult to pay attention to the Scripture readings and homily while holding a crying or restless child in church. While it may initially seem odd for a relative or friend to take the child to a separate place during the Liturgy of the Word at the child's baptism, this gesture reflects the value that the Church places on the Scripture as a source of formation for the parents, the godparents, and other members of the assembly.

The Baptismal Font

The third procession in the baptismal liturgy takes the parents and their child and the godparents to the baptismal font, which "is a symbol of both tomb and womb; its power is the power of the triumphant cross; and baptism sets the Christian on the path to the life that will never end, the 'eighth day' of eternity where Christ's reign of peace and justice is celebrated."[17] The dual image of "tomb and womb" acknowledges the reality that those who make the journey to and through the waters of the baptismal font undertake a way of life that is marked by dying and rising, death and new life. For the child to be baptized, that is the path that Christ holds open going forward, while the parents, godparents, and others in the assembly are already on that path and can recognize in this imagery experiences of dying and rising that have already unfolded in their lives. For the parents in particular, the font as image of "tomb and womb" serves to acknowledge that their journey to God going forward will be marked by the inevitable moments of dying and rising that come with parenting and their promise to "bring them [their children] up in the faith."[18] At a time when fewer parents are making this promise, it is all the more important that other members of the local

---

15. OBC, 17.
16. OBC, 14.
17. *Built of Living Stones: Art, Architecture, and Worship* (BLS), 68.
18. OBC, 56.

church community be present at the baptism to assure the parents that they will have support in their role as Christian parents.

The Altar

"The baptismal font and its location reflect the Christian's journey *through* the waters of baptism *to* the altar,"[19] and so the next procession moves from the font to the altar where, in time, the children who have been baptized "will share at the table of his [the Lord's] Sacrifice, / and will call upon God as Father in the midst of the Church."[20] In the ancient Church, newly baptized children participated in Communion during their baptismal liturgy, and that practice has continued in many Eastern Christian churches; but in the Roman Catholic Church, Communion for children usually follows baptism by a few years. So, while the children will not receive Communion at their baptismal liturgy, they are still brought to the altar to signify the next milestone on their journey as new Christians.

One of the reasons why the *Order of Baptism of Children* recommends celebrating baptism within Mass is "so that the connection between Baptism and the Most Holy Eucharist may stand out more clearly."[21] For the parents, godparents, and others in the assembly, participating in the Eucharist and receiving Communion at the baptismal liturgy is a reminder that the Eucharist "nourishes the disciple with Christ's Body and Blood for his transformation in Christ."[22] When baptism is celebrated within Mass, the procession to the altar reaches its fulfillment as the parents, godparents, and other members of the assembly are nourished with Christ's Body and Blood for the ongoing journey to God that began with their baptism.

From the altar, the final procession of the baptismal liturgy takes the parents and their newly baptized child, the godparents, and other members of the assembly out into the world "as baptized disciples sent to act on behalf of those in need and to tend to God's creation."[23] The parents are sent to continue their journey to God as "the first witnesses of the faith to their children," while all in the assembly are encouraged

---

19. BLS, 66.
20. OBC, 68.
21. OBC, 9.
22. CCC, 1275.
23. Mary A. Ehle, *Baptized for Discipleship: The Meaning of Baptism for Our Christian Life* (Chicago: LTP, 2019), 28.

to "be active members of his [God's] people."[24] The deacon gives voice to the meaning of this final procession in the words of the dismissal: "Go and announce the Gospel of the Lord," "Go in peace, glorifying the Lord by your life."[25]

Reflection Questions

1. How have you experienced the love and help of the Christian community in your journey of faith?

2. In your ministry as a deacon, how can you help parents to experience the love and help of the parish community during their preparation for baptism and during the celebration of baptism?

3. Which of the four stations of the baptismal liturgy and which of the processions to and from these stations resonate most strongly with your journey to God? Which do you need to be more attentive to in your discipleship and in your leadership at the celebration of baptism?

Water: Opening Us to Holiness and Joining Us to the Paschal Mystery

Catholic liturgies are rich in symbolism. "Jesus himself used physical signs to manifest his union with the Father and to reveal his mission to the world,"[26] and the Church has continuously used gestures, language, and actions in liturgy to express and develop the relationship between Christians and God. Words are an important tool in understanding and expressing faith, but words alone cannot capture the fullness of the Christian life. "Since human beings on this earth are always made of flesh and blood, they not only will and think, but also speak and sing, move and celebrate."[27] The baptismal liturgy brings together words and physical signs to manifest what occurs in baptism, and the most important of these signs is water.

Many ancient people believed that water was one of the four elements that made up the universe, the other three being earth, air,

---

24. OBC, 70.
25. *The Roman Missal* (RM), The Order of Mass, 144.
26. BLS, 25.
27. BLS, 24.

and fire. In the Judeo-Christian tradition, water appears as one of the original elements of creation in the first sentence of the Bible: "In the beginning when God created the heavens and the earth, the earth was a formless void and darkness covered the face of the deep, while a wind from God swept over the face of the waters."[28] Throughout the pages of the Bible, water plays a major role in the formation of God's holy people, as is seen in the prayer for the blessing of water and invocation of God over the water in the *Order of Baptism of Children*:

> O God, who by invisible power
> accomplish a wondrous effect
> through sacramental signs
> and who in many ways have prepared water, your creation,
> to show forth the grace of Baptism;
>
> O God, whose Spirit
> in the first moments of the world's creation
> hovered over the waters,
> so that the very substance of water
> would even then take to itself the power to sanctify;
>
> O God, who by the outpouring of the flood
> foreshadowed regeneration,
> so that from the mystery of one and the same element of water
> would come an end to vice and a beginning of virtue;
>
> O God, who caused the children of Abraham
> to pass dry-shod through the Red Sea,
> so that the chosen people,
> set free from slavery to Pharaoh,
> would prefigure the people of the baptized;
>
> O God, whose Son,
> baptized by John in the waters of the Jordan,
> was anointed with the Holy Spirit,
> and, as he hung upon the Cross,
> gave forth water from his side along with blood,

---

28. Genesis 1:1–2.

and after his Resurrection, commanded his disciples:
"Go forth, teach all nations, baptizing them
in the name of the Father and of the Son and of the Holy Spirit,"
look now, we pray, upon the face of your Church
and graciously unseal for her the fountain of Baptism.

May this water receive by the Holy Spirit
the grace of your Only Begotten Son,
so that human nature, created in your image
and washed clean through the Sacrament of Baptism
from all the squalor of the life of old,
may be found worthy to rise to the life of newborn children
through water and the Holy Spirit.

May the power of the Holy Spirit,
O Lord, we pray,
come down through your Son
into the fullness of this font,
so that all who have been buried with Christ
by Baptism into death
may rise again to life with him.
Who lives and reigns for ever and ever.
Amen.[29]

If you have proclaimed this prayer at many baptisms and now find
yourself rushing through it because it is too familiar, take a few moments
to ponder the text slowly. If the text is relatively new to you, read it
prayerfully a few times. In the style of lectio divina, contemplate one
or more of the images of water in this prayer for a period of time. The
prayer literally follows the flow of water from creation through baptism
and shows how each major appearance of water in the Bible foreshadowed
its use in baptism. The prayer "is a confession of faith in the God of
the ages, acclaiming what he has done in former times, confident of his
love being effective now, and looking forward to the resurrection which
will be the joyful lot of all who are buried, through baptism, with Christ
in death."[30] We turn now to some of those images.

---

29. OBC, 54.
30. Mark Searle, *Christening: The Making of Christians* (Collegeville, MN: Liturgical Press, 1980), 70–71.

A Rich Symbol of Grace

Think of the classic definition of sacraments as "efficacious signs of grace, instituted by Christ and entrusted to the Church, by which divine life is dispensed to us,"[31] and then consider how such a common element as water becomes "a rich symbol of the grace"[32] that God gives us in the sacrament of baptism. From the repertoire of church music, see how John Newton, who is most famous for writing the lyrics of "Amazing Grace," wrote about water as a sign of grace in another hymn:

> See! the streams of living waters,
> Springing from eternal love,
> Well supply thy sons and daughters,
> And all fear of want remove.
> Who can faint, when such a river
> Ever will their thirst assuage?
> Grace, which, like the Lord, the giver,
> Never fails from age to age.[33]

As you consider your experience of God's grace, think about how the natural characteristics of water deepen your understanding of that experience: water nurtures and sustains life, water refreshes, water purifies, water quenches thirst, water rains down on people, water moves people in a different direction, water overwhelms, water revives.

A Wellspring of Holiness

After speaking of water as showing "forth the grace of Baptism," the prayer goes on to proclaim how the Spirit "hovered over the waters" at creation "so that the very substance of water / would even then take to itself the power to sanctify." From the dawn of creation, God intended water to be not just the source and sustenance of natural life, but the "wellspring of all holiness,"[34] providing source and sustenance for those who respond to God's call to holiness. Those who pass through the waters of baptism become children of God "and partakers of the divine nature, and so are truly sanctified. They must therefore hold on to and

---

31. CCC, 1131.
32. CCC, 1217.
33. "Glorious Things of Thee Are Spoken."
34. CCC, 1218.

perfect in their lives that holiness which they have received from God."[35]
As you consider your call to holiness in baptism and your ongoing
response to that call, reflect on this fifth-century inscription in the
baptistery of the Basilica of St. John Lateran in Rome:

> Here is born in Spirit-soaked fertility
> a brood destined for another City,
> begotten by God's blowing
> and borne upon this torrent
> by the Church their virgin mother.
> Reborn in these depths they reach for heaven's realm,
> the born-but-once unknown by felicity.
> This spring is life that floods the world,
> the wounds of Christ its awesome source.
> Sinner sink beneath this sacred surf
> that swallows age and spits up youth.
> Sinner here scour sin away down to innocence,
> for they know no enmity who are by
> one font, one Spirit, one faith made one.
> Sinner shudder not at sin's kind and number,
> for those born here are holy.[36]

A New Beginning of Goodness

As the prayer for the blessing of water continues, it speaks of how the
flood described in Genesis 6—9 "foreshadowed regeneration" and
brought "an end to vice and a beginning of virtue." The waters of the
flood covered the earth and brought death to all living things except
those on the ark. When the waters receded, new life emerged. In the
same way, the waters of baptism "make an end of sin and a new beginning
of goodness."[37] The waters of the flood enrich our understanding of the
Paschal Mystery, that is, Christ's work of redemption accomplished
principally by his "Passion, Resurrection from the dead, and glorious
Ascension, whereby 'dying he destroyed our death, rising he restored our

---

35. LG, 40.
36. Quoted in Aidan Kavanagh, *The Shape of Baptism: The Rite of Christian Initiation* (New York: Pueblo Publishing Company, 1978), 49.
37. CCC, 1219.

life."[38] The waters of baptism incorporate us into the Body of Christ, that is, the Church, by uniting us to the paschal mystery: "Those who are baptized are united with Christ in a death like his, are buried with him in death, and also in him are given life and are raised up. For in Baptism, nothing other than the Paschal Mystery is recalled and accomplished, because in it human beings pass from the death of sin into life."[39] The very term *baptism* comes from the Greek word *baptizein*, which "means to 'plunge' or 'immerse'; the 'plunge' into the water symbolizes the catechumen's burial into Christ's death, from which he rises up by resurrection with him, as 'a new creature.'"[40] This is why the Church prefers immersion for the baptism of children as well as adults as "more suitably signifies participation in the Death and Resurrection of Christ."[41]

An Image of God's Holy People

The story from Exodus of Israel's passage through the waters of the Red Sea also appears in the prayer, and the liberated children of Abraham are said to "prefigure the people of the baptized." Centuries ago, St. Cyril catechized with a parallel of Moses delivering the Israelites and Christ's saving sinners: "As Moses was appointed to lead his afflicted people from Egypt, so Christ came to deliver the people of the world who were overcome by sin."[42] When baptism is celebrated at the Easter Vigil, the proclamation of the Exodus story during the Liturgy of the Word is especially poignant as a foreshadowing of the liberation from sin that occurs in baptism. Even when baptism is celebrated at other times and the Exodus story is not part of the Liturgy of the Word, this image testifies that those who are baptized are part of God's holy people who are no longer slaves to sin. Mark Searle draws on such an image when he likens the baptized to the chosen people: "The Church is the new Israel of God (Galatians 6:16), a people he has redeemed for himself, and all who belong to it must have passed through the waters of deliverance."[43] This not only is good news for the one being baptized but also reminds the parents, godparents, and other baptized members of the assembly

38. CCC, 1067.
39. CI, 6.
40. CCC, 1214.
41. CI, 22.
42. Cyril of Jerusalem, *Mystagogic Catecheses* 1:3 in Edward Yarnold, *The Awe-Inspiring Rites of Initiation: The Origins of the R.C.I.A.* (Collegeville, MN: Liturgical Press, 1994), 71.
43. Searle, *Christening*, 73.

that the experiences of sin and death that they face throughout their lives can always give way to freedom and new life.

Water in Jesus' Life and Teaching

Three references to water in the life and teaching of Jesus appear in the prayer. First is his baptism at the hands of John the Baptist when Jesus "identifies himself thoroughly with us in answering John the Baptist's call to repentance."[44] As Jesus emerged from the waters of the Jordan, "The Spirit who had hovered over the waters of the first creation descended then on the Christ as a prelude of the new creation."[45] Jesus was, in the words of the prayer, "anointed with the Holy Spirit" for his mission that led to suffering and death. Those who are baptized are joined to this mission and to the pattern of dying and rising. The second reference is to the water that flowed along with blood from the side of Jesus as he hung upon the cross. The Church has seen this as an image of the sacraments of baptism (water) and Eucharist (blood) through which people are joined to Christ and nourished for lives of Christian discipleship. The third reference draws on the commission that appears at the end of Matthew's Gospel. It is not only a commission to teach and baptize but, as the Greek text of this passage indicates, a commission to "'go and make disciples of all nations,' which better expresses what it means to render to Christ the obedience of faith. Baptism goes, not with simply being taught, but with becoming a disciple of the Lord, a follower heart and soul."[46]

The Spirit Moving over the Water

The last two paragraphs of the prayer take us from God's use of water in the past to the present moment of baptism. Confident that God has brought about great things through water in the past, we invoke the Holy Spirit to come down on the water with power "so that all who have been buried with Christ / by Baptism into death / may rise again to life with him." Here, the text is accompanied by an action, as the rite indicates that "the celebrant touches the water with his right hand."[47] As the priest or deacon touches the water, "the water moves, ripples with

---

44. Searle, *Christening*, 74.
45. CCC, 1224.
46. Searle, *Christening*, 75.
47. OBC, 54.

life and energy as the Spirit passes over."[48] Marty Haugen captures this
in the refrain of "Song over the Waters": "God, you have moved upon
the waters, / you have sung in the rush of wind and flame; / and in your
love, you have called us sons and daughters, / make us people of the water
and your name."[49]

Water in the Celebration of Baptism

The prayer for the blessing of water and invocation of God over the water
is the longest prayer text in the *Order of Baptism of Children*. If baptism
is celebrated within Mass, the only prayer text that is longer is the
Eucharistic Prayer. This length gives an indication of the importance
of the prayer to the baptismal liturgy. The prayer's extensive references
to water make it clear that water is an essential and powerful sign in
the celebration of baptism. Yet, just as familiarity with this prayer may
incline us to rush through its proclamation, our inclination to keep
things simple may move us to minimize the use of water when presiding
at the celebration of baptism. Father Robert Hovda, a leader in the
liturgical movement after the Second Vatican Council, wrote:

> I remember a pamphlet on baptism which contained innumerable
> suggestions for the celebration of that rite but did not once mention
> the actual bathing in water. To miss the point of a thing—that
> totally takes some doing. Immersion in baptism, conviction and
> reaching out to the hearers in the proclamation of the word, eating
> from the common plate and drinking from the common cup—
> these are essentials. Start with them! Don't leave the shriveled
> and neglected essential elements untouched while concentrating
> on the periphery![50]

The Catholic bishops of the United States express a similar sentiment
in writing, "Poorly utilized or minimal signs do not enliven the community's faith and can even diminish active participation."[51] When water
is extolled as it is in the blessing prayer and then followed by pouring
a few scant drops of water on the child's head, the priest or deacon has
yielded to the temptation to use a "poorly utilized or minimal sign."

---

48. Searle, *Christening*, 76.
49. "Song over the Waters," by Marty Haugen. Copyright © 1987 GIA Publications, Inc. All rights reserved. Used by permission.
50. Robert Hovda, "The Amen Corner," *Worship* 61, no. 1 (1987): 79.
51. BLS, 26.

As deacons, we need to become comfortable in our use of water during the celebration of baptism. If we have never considered celebrating baptism by immersion, perhaps we need to reflect on why we avoid this form of baptism, which the Church says "more suitably signifies participation in the Death and Resurrection of Christ."[52] Many of us are fathers and have a lot of experience with bathing children, so lowering a child into water is something that should come naturally to us. Doing this in a baptismal font may take some practice, but those communities where baptism by immersion is done regularly have found it well worth the extra effort. Even when we baptize by pouring water, which is certainly permitted and valid, we can be generous in the amount of water we use.

> *How* we baptize, *where* we baptize and *what* we use—the sacramental signs—will reveal either God's gracious love or something else. A passive assembly, graceless gestures, a minimum of water, a dab of chrism—all reveal that we don't believe this child is important, this baptism is significant, or this community is worthy of the effort that a fuller celebration requires. It's the difference between a peck on the cheek and a kiss on the lips. No pecks, please! God has acted so generously toward us. Dare we be stingy with the signs of divine love? Dare we skimp when it comes to the signs that save us? A good celebration of baptism requires the full use of its sacramental signs.[53]

Reflection Questions

1. In your ministry as a deacon, how do you respond to your baptismal call to holiness? How have you experienced dying and rising in your life and ministry?

2. Which of the images of water from the blessing of water and invocation of God over the water resonates most strongly with your experience of baptism and discipleship?

3. How might you incorporate the images of water from this prayer in your preaching at the celebration of baptism?

---

52. CI, 22.
53. David Philippart, "Grace through Sacramental Signs," in *Catechesis and Mystagogy: Infant Baptism* (Chicago: LTP, 1996), 71.

4. If your use of water during the celebration of baptism tends to be minimal, how might you move to a fuller use of this sacramental sign? If you have never celebrated baptism by immersion, what fears or other obstacles do you need to confront?

Anointing: What It Means to Be a Priest, Prophet, and King

The anointing with sacred chrism after baptism is another gesture that has great symbolic importance. It is the first of four explanatory rites that further break open the meaning of the baptism that has just taken place. This anointing is unique to the baptism of children; when adults and children of catechetical age are baptized, the anointing associated with the sacrament of confirmation is done after the baptism. Prior to anointing the child on the crown of his or her head, the priest or deacon prays:

> Almighty God, the Father of our Lord Jesus Christ,
> has freed you from sin,
> given you new birth by water and the Holy Spirit,
> and joined you to his people.
> He now anoints you with the Chrism of salvation,
> so that you may remain members of Christ, Priest,
>   Prophet and King,
> unto eternal life.[54]

The images in the first sentence echo themes that appeared in the prayer for the blessing of water and invocation of God over the water. What is new in the prayer is the threefold image of "Priest, Prophet and King" that appears in the second sentence. Those who are baptized are joined to Christ, who "is the one whom the Father anointed with the Holy Spirit and established as priest, prophet, and king. The whole people of God participates in these three offices of Christ and bears the responsibilities for mission and service that flow from them."[55] The word *Christ* literally means "the anointed one," and so this anointing after baptism identifies the one who is baptized with Christ, his mission, and his life of the Spirit. "The anointing with perfumed oil is the joyful acknowledgement

---

54. OBC, 62.
55. CCC, 783.

that we are one with Christ, living members of his body, members through whom he continues to live in the world and to act among us for our salvation and for the Father's glory."[56]

How can we break open this image of priest, prophet, and king in our understanding, in catechesis with parents and godparents, and in preaching at the celebration of baptism? Pope Francis summarized all three elements of this image when he said, "To participate in the royal and prophetic priesthood of Christ . . . means making of oneself an offering acceptable to God (see Romans 12:1), bearing witness to him through a life of faith and charity (see *Lumen gentium*, n. 12), placing it at the service of others, after the example of the Lord Jesus (see Matthew 20:25–28; John 13:13–17)."[57] Let's look at each of the three elements of this image.

Priest: The common use of the word *priest* to refer to ordained priests and our respect for the unique ministry of ordained priests may lead us to overlook the fact that "the whole Church is a priestly people. Through Baptism all the faithful share in the priesthood of Christ. This participation is called the 'common priesthood of the faithful.'"[58] When we gather for liturgy, it is this priesthood of believers that celebrates and presents itself as "an eternal offering"[59] to God. Beyond the liturgy, this priesthood of believers lives "as priestly people when we reflect on how we make present the holiness and sacredness that is inside of us and then act accordingly. When we honor the holiness and sacredness in every man, woman, and child we encounter by speaking words that build others up rather than tear them down, we acknowledge the holiness within all God's people. When we lead prayer in our communities, in small groups, in our homes, and among our friends, we embody our identity as members of God's priestly people."[60]

Prophet: In common parlance, a prophet is one who proclaims what will take place in the future. In the Catholic tradition, however, a prophet is one whose developed understanding of the faith makes him or her "Christ's witness in the midst of this world"[61] in the present. The task of the prophet is "to communicate God's message for *now*, and to

56. Searle, *Christening*, 99.
57. Pope Francis, General Audience, May 9, 2018.
58. CCC, 1591.
59. RM, Eucharistic Prayer III, 113.
60. Ehle, *Baptized*, 14.
61. CCC, 785.

summon the people to respond *today*."[62] The prophetic character that baptism conveys can be challenging, as it forces us to examine how our lives are or are not witnessing to Christ and his Gospel, and as it moves us in love to invite others to join in building up the reign of God in a world that falls short of God's vision for the kingdom.

King: To understand what it is to be a king in the Christian sense, look at the Gospel readings for the Solemnity of Our Lord Jesus Christ, King of the Universe. In Year A, the Son of Man renders judgment based on the principle "whatsoever you did for one of the least brothers of mine, you did for me."[63] In Year B, Jesus tells Pilate that his "kingdom does not belong to this world,"[64] and in Year C, the repentant criminal hanging next to Jesus says, "remember me when you come into your Kingdom."[65] Christian kingship is modeled not on its regal counterpart in this world but on the vision of God's kingdom, where serving others and repentance are regal values. "For the Christian, 'to reign is to serve him,' particularly when serving 'the poor and the suffering, in whom the Church recognizes the image of her poor and suffering founder.'"[66]

Anointing in the Celebration of Baptism

The way in which we use the sacred chrism during the celebration of baptism should reflect the importance of the anointing and the related images of priest, prophet, and king. This anointing is "on the crown of his [her] head"[67] to signify "the royal priesthood of the baptized and enrollment into the company of the People of God."[68] Using an ample amount of the chrism honors the baptismal status of the child and allows all in the assembly to both see and smell the scented oil.

> The better the anointing, the more loudly God speaks *to the church* about belonging to Christ. Oil is to be poured out on each child's head and rubbed in. The whole top of the head is to be rubbed with the scented Chrism. This is to be a lavish anointing, not a miserly afterthought. The oil is poured out and rubbed in;

---

62. Bernhard W. Anderson, *Understanding the Old Testament*, 3rd ed. (Englewood Cliffs, NJ: Prentice-Hall, Inc., 1975), 227.
63. *Lectionary for Mass* (LM), 160.
64. LM, 161.
65. LM, 162.
66. CCC, 786.
67. OBC, 62.
68. OBC, 18.3.

a dab of oil on the presider's thumb, smudged on the forehead (as is often done) and then wiped off doesn't even come close.[69]

Here again, the experience that many of us have as fathers is relevant. We have rubbed oil on our children's bodies after bathing them. We know how it can soothe them and we know how wonderful it makes them smell. How much more important it is to let each baptized child bear "the aroma of Christ to God"[70] by our generous use of the sacred chrism for this anointing.

Reflection Questions

1. In your ministry as a deacon, how have you incorporated the roles of priest, prophet, and king that were bestowed on you in baptism?

2. How might you share what it means to be a priest, prophet, and king in catechesis with parents and in preaching at the celebration of baptism?

3. If your use of the sacred chrism during the celebration of baptism tends to be minimal, how might you move to a fuller use of the sacramental sign?

Lighted Candle: Becoming the Light of Christ for the World

The handing on of a lighted candle is the third of the four explanatory rites that follow baptism. Taking the paschal candle, the priest or deacon says, "Receive the light of Christ," and then a member of the family lights a candle from the paschal candle. The priest or deacon then says:

> Parents and godparents,
> this light is entrusted to you to be kept burning brightly,
> so that your children, enlightened by Christ,
> may walk always as children of the light
> and, persevering in the faith,

---

69. Timothy Fitzgerald, *Infant Baptism: A Parish Celebration* (Chicago: LTP, 1994), 55–56.
70. 2 Corinthians 2:15.

Through baptism, children become bearers of the light of Christ.

may run to meet the Lord when he comes
with all the Saints in the heavenly court.[71]

Light is a pervasive image in the Bible. It first appears in chapter 1
of Genesis (1:14–19) and then appears in numerous other books of the
Old and New Testaments. In the New Testament, light prominently
refers to Christ, as in the first chapter of John's Gospel: "What has come
into being in him was life, and the life was the light of all people. The
light shines in the darkness, and the darkness did not overcome it."[72]
Jesus used light as an image to describe his followers: "You are the light
of the world. A city built on a hill cannot be hid. No one after lighting
a lamp puts it under the bushel basket, but on the lampstand, and it
gives light to all in the house. In the same way, let your light shine before
others, so that they may see your good works and give glory to your

71. OBC, 64.
72. John 1:4–5.

Father in heaven."[73] Scripture uses light as an image both for Christ and for those who follow Christ, and, correspondingly, the rite of handing on a lighted candle in the baptismal liturgy connects this twofold imagery of light by entrusting the light of the paschal candle (which refers to Christ) to the parents so that their "children, enlightened by Christ, / may walk always as children of the light." Just as through baptism the children become part of the Body of Christ, so they also become bearers of the light that is Christ.

Enlightened by Christ

The term "enlightened by Christ" has ancient roots. "The proper name for the newly baptized is 'neophytes,' meaning 'the newly enlightened.' This name derives, clearly, from the Greek-speaking Churches, where those preparing for baptism are called *photizomenoi*, 'those to be enlightened.'"[74] When the one being baptized is an adult who has moved from the darkness of sin to a life illuminated by the light of Christ, it can be easy to recognize this sense of enlightenment. In these cases, "the 'enlightenment' of baptism is not a flickering flame but a burst of God's glory in those whose capacities to receive it had been expanded to their utmost."[75] In the baptism of children, the light of Christ is entrusted to the parents "to be kept burning brightly" and to be shared with the child as he or she grows. As the flame of a candle starts small and then grows stronger and brighter, so the light of Christ grows stronger and brighter when a child who has been enlightened by Christ in baptism grows in faith.

Walk Always as Children of the Light

The prayer for the handing on of a lighted candle echoes St. Paul's encouragement to the followers of Christ to "Live as children of light—for the fruit of the light is found in all that is good and right and true."[76] Like the lamp that is not to be hidden but is to give light to others, those who have been enlightened by Christ are to share that light with others. "Walking as a disciple of Christ is an active pursuit. It is a journey in which the voices of Christians offer the light of hope in places where

---

73. Matthew 5:14–16.
74. Searle, *Christening*, 102.
75. Aidan Kavanagh in *A Baptism Sourcebook* (Chicago: LTP, 1993), 193.
76. Ephesians 5:8–9.

darkness seems impenetrable. As Jesus lifted up the oppressed, so we too must do the same in the twenty-first century. Through our voices and actions we reveal the power of the Light of Christ."[77] Our credibility as children of the light depends on our willingness to shine the light of Christ wherever darkness exists, especially insofar as it brings light to the darkness in which others live.

Persevering in the Faith

An increasingly large number of Catholics who were baptized as children become disaffiliated from their faith before they celebrate confirmation.[78] While the phrase "persevering in the faith" may flow easily from our mouths as we proclaim the prayer for handing on a lighted candle, doing so is a challenge for many. By way of assurance, the Bible is full of examples of how this has been the case throughout the ages. The Bible also assures us that God has provided light to guide those who are struggling and searching. When the Israelites cried to God for help during their slavery in Egypt, "the angel of the LORD appeared to [Moses] in a flame of fire out of a bush."[79] After their release from the bondage of Egypt, God led the Israelites as "a pillar of fire by night, to give them light."[80] The psalmist sings, "The LORD is my light and my salvation; / whom shall I fear?"[81] To those who were following him, Jesus said, "I am the light of the world. Whoever follows me will never walk in darkness but will have the light of life."[82] Every person faces struggles and every person seeks meaning in life. In baptism, we are given the light of Christ to help us through our struggles and to find the ultimate meaning in our life. In our catechesis and preaching for baptism, let us assure parents and others that, while the world's alluring lights will eventually burn out, Christ, the true light, will stay with us always. As St. John Henry Newman prayed:

---

77. Ehle, *Baptized*, 21–22.
78. See, for example, *Going, Going, Gone: The Dynamics of Disaffiliation in Young Catholics* (Winona, MN: St. Mary's Press, 2018).
79. Exodus 3:2.
80. Exodus 13:21.
81. Psalm 27:1.
82. John 8:12.

Lead, Kindly Light, amid the encircling gloom

Lead Thou me on!

The night is dark, and I am far from home—

Lead Thou me on![83]

The Lighted Candle in the Celebration of Baptism

Our use of the lighted candle in the celebration of baptism should reflect the importance of the image of light in the Christian life. The candle is lit from the paschal candle. The size and design of the paschal candle ought to be worthy of the great symbolism that this candle conveys: "the light of Christ rising in glory dispel the darkness of our hearts and minds."[84] The paschal candles in many churches are simply too small to bear the weight of this great symbolism. If that is the case in your church, it may be time to begin a conversation with the pastor about investing in a more significant paschal candle and stand. The candle that is lit from the paschal candle and then given to the parents also symbolizes the light of Christ. It needs to be larger than a taper. A candle that is at least one inch in diameter, several inches tall, and able to stand on its own in a base or candleholder works well. The size and significance of the candle are more important than any additional images that are applied to it. If the candle has a stand, it can be left burning until the end of the baptismal liturgy, perhaps next to the paschal candle or the baptismal font. Encourage the parents to light the candle again each year on the child's birthday and baptismal anniversary.

Reflection Questions

1. How has the light of Christ shone in times of darkness that you have experienced in your life?

2. Who are some people who have borne the light of Christ to you?

3. If the paschal candle and baptismal candles in your church are too small to convey the importance of the image of Christ the light, how might you move to a fuller use of these sacramental signs?

---

83. *The Pillar of the Cloud.*
84. RM, The Easter Vigil in the Holy Night, 14.

PART 2

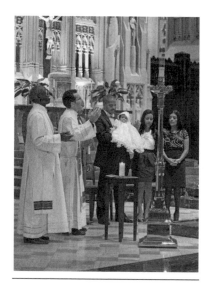

Baptizing with Style and Grace

Chapter 3

A Fully Celebrated Ritual

As deacons who preside and assist at the celebration of baptism, we honor the Church's rich theology of baptism when we help people to experience it in the baptismal liturgy. As noted in the previous chapter, the celebration of baptism is the place where most people will encounter what the Church believes and teaches about baptism. For us as deacons and for our colleagues in pastoral ministry, this implies that it is critical to prepare and celebrate the liturgy of baptism well. My friend and mentor Father Larry Madden, sj, a noted liturgist and pastor, devoted much of his ministry to what he called "the doing of liturgy." He believed, as do I, that well-prepared and well-celebrated liturgies have a tremendous capacity to lead people into deep encounters with their faith. A few months before he died, he wrote, "If we add quality preaching and a reverent enactment of the rites by the various ministers to beautiful and appropriate music, I believe some people's symbolic, poetic capacities can be awakened and they can be seduced into experiences of the Paschal mystery."[1]

In 2020, the Catholic Church in the United States began using a revised ritual book for the baptism of children: the *Order of Baptism of Children*. While the revised rite for baptism does not introduce significant changes to the rite that had been in use for fifty years,[2] it provides an opportunity to revisit the elements that go into a full and beautiful celebration of baptism. If we believe that "Holy Baptism is the basis of the whole Christian life,"[3] then it is well worth our time and effort to prepare and celebrate it well.

---

1. "Parish Liturgy during the Past Twenty Years from a Pastor's Viewpoint," *Liturgical Ministry* (Winter 2011): 43.
2. *Rite of Baptism for Children*.
3. CCC, 1213.

The Assembly

One of the guiding principles of Catholic liturgy, as enunciated by
the Second Vatican Council, is that "liturgical services are not private
functions, but are celebrations belonging to the Church, which is the
'sacrament of unity,' namely, the holy people united and ordered under
their bishops. . . . Whenever rites, according to their specific nature,
make provision for communal celebration involving the presence and
active participation of the faithful, it is to be stressed that this way of
celebrating them is to be preferred, as far as possible, to a celebration that
is individual and, so to speak, private."[4] The *Order of Baptism of Children*
applies this principle to the celebration of baptism when it states:

> In the celebration of Baptism, the People of God—represented
> not only by godparents, parents, and relatives, but also, insofar as
> possible, by friends, acquaintances, neighbors, and some members
> of the local Church—should take an active part, in order to show
> their common faith and to express their shared joy with which the
> newly baptized are received into the Church.[5]

> The People of God, that is the Church represented by the local
> community, plays just as important a part in the Baptism of
> children as in that of adults. . . . The community exercises its
> function when, together with the celebrant, it expresses its consent
> after the profession of faith by the parents and godparents. In this
> way, it becomes apparent that the faith in which the children are
> being baptized is a treasure not belonging to the family alone, but
> to the whole Church of Christ.[6]

It cannot be any clearer: the norm for the baptismal liturgy in the Catholic
Church is a celebration with an assembly of people that includes more
than just the family and friends of the child being baptized.

Scheduling the Celebration of Baptism

If a fully celebrated baptismal liturgy calls for the participation of the
parish community, then a primary consideration is to schedule baptisms

---

4. *Constitution on the Sacred Liturgy* (CSL), 26–27.
5. CI, 7.
6. OBC, 4.

The readings on a number of Sundays throughout the year speak specifically about baptism and the call to follow Christ.

for those times when members of the parish community are able to participate. The most natural time for that is at Sunday Mass. If anything has a right and a reason to be incorporated into Sunday Mass, it is the celebration of baptism, as noted in the *Order of Baptism of Children*:

> To illustrate the paschal character of Baptism, it is recommended that the Sacrament be celebrated at the Easter Vigil or on a Sunday, when the Church commemorates the Resurrection of the Lord. Furthermore, on a Sunday, Baptism may be celebrated also within Mass, so that the whole community may be able to take part in the rite and so that the connection between Baptism and the Most Holy Eucharist may stand out more clearly.[7]

While some parishes have had success with incorporating the baptism of children in the Easter Vigil, others focus on the Christian initiation

---

7. OBC, 9.

of adults at the Easter Vigil and celebrate the baptism of children on Easter Sunday and other appropriate Sundays.

Celebrating baptism within Sunday Mass calls for careful preparation, starting with the choice of the Sundays on which baptism will be celebrated. The rite warns that "this should not happen too often,"[8] so the first issue is how often your parish needs to celebrate baptism. A small parish with very few baptisms and just one Sunday Mass may only need to schedule baptism two or three times a year, while a large parish with many baptisms and several Sunday Masses may need to schedule baptism several times a year, rotating the celebration of baptism among the various Sunday Masses. In either case, baptism is not celebrated at any particular Sunday Mass too often over the course of a year.

Scheduling baptism on a given Sunday each month is a common practice in some places, but that can leave some homilists wondering how to connect the baptism with the Scripture readings of the day. While the rite allows one or more of the readings from the "Conferral of Infant Baptism" section of the *Lectionary for Mass* to replace the readings of the day,[9] an alternative practice is to look to the *Lectionary for Mass* and the liturgical year for Sundays when the readings and the season provide a fitting context for the celebration of baptism. "The liturgical year and the lectionary already provide an ample framework for the public celebration of baptism. Rather than accommodating baptism on random Sundays, then shaping the lectionary to fit the schedule, parish communities would be better served by letting the lectionary and the calendar shape them and their rhythms of initiation."[10] The readings on any Sunday provide opportunities to preach about discipleship, but the readings on certain Sundays speak more explicitly about baptism and the call to follow Christ. While this is not an exhaustive list, some examples of appropriate Sundays include the following:

- *Epiphany:* "Your light has come" (Isaiah 60:1–6). "The Gentiles are coheirs, members of the same body" (Ephesians 3:2–3a, 5–6).

- *Baptism of the Lord:* "A light for the nations" (Isaiah 42:1–4, 6–7, Year A). "Jesus was baptized" (Matthew 3:13–17, Year A). "Come to the water" (Isaiah 55:1–11, Year B). "You will draw water joyfully" (Isaiah 12:2–3, 4bcd, 5–6, Year B). "He will baptize you with the Holy Spirit"

---

8. OBC, 9.
9. LM, 756–760; OBC, 29.2a.
10. Timothy Fitzgerald, *Infant Baptism: A Parish Celebration* (Chicago: LTP, 1994), 74.

(Mark 1:7–11, Year B). "He saved us through the bath of rebirth" (Titus 2:11–14; 3:4–7, Year C). "He will baptize you with the Holy Spirit and fire" (Luke 3:15–16, 21–22, Year C).

- *Fifth Sunday in Ordinary Time:* "Your light shall break forth like the dawn" (Isaiah 58:7–10, Year A). "The just man is a light in darkness" (Psalm 112:4–5, 6–7, 8–9, Year A). "You are the light of the world" (Matthew 5:13–16, Year A). "Here I am . . . send me" (Isaiah 6:1–2a, 3–8, Year C). "From now on you will be catching men" (Luke 5:1–11, Year C).

- *Seventh Sunday in Ordinary Time:* "The one . . . who anointed us is God" (2 Corinthians 1:18–22, Year B).

- *Tenth Sunday in Ordinary Time:* "He [Jesus] said to him, 'Follow me'" (Matthew 9:9–13, Year A).

- Easter Sunday: "Everyone who believes in him will receive forgiveness of sins" (Acts 10:34a, 37–43). "You have died, and your life is hidden with Christ in God" (Colossians 3:1–4). "He had to rise from the dead" (John 20:1–9).

- *Second Sunday of Easter:* "Gave us a new birth to a living hope" (1 Peter 1:3–9, Year A). "Blessed are those who have not seen and have believed" (John 20:19–31).

- *Fourth Sunday of Easter:* "Repent and be baptized, every one of you, in the name of Jesus Christ" (Acts 2:14a, 36–41, Year A). "We are God's children now" (1 John 3:1–2, Year B). "I have made you a light to the Gentiles" (Acts 13:14, 43–52, Year C). "My sheep hear my voice . . . and they follow me" (John 10:27–30, Year C).

- *Fifth Sunday of Easter:* "You are 'a chosen race, a royal priesthood'" (1 Peter 2:4–9, Year A). "I am the vine, you are the branches" (John 15:1–8, Year B).

- *Sixth Sunday of Easter:* "Can anyone withhold the water for baptizing these people?" (Acts 10:25–26, 34–35, 44–48, Year B). "It was not you who chose me, but I who chose you" (John 15:9–17, Year B).

- *Ascension of the Lord (in dioceses where it is celebrated on a Sunday):* "You will be baptized with the Holy Spirit" (Acts 1:1–11). "May the eyes of your hearts be enlightened" (Ephesians 1:17–23, Year A). "Make disciples of all nations, baptizing them" (Matthew 28:16–20, Year A). "One Lord, one faith, one baptism" (Ephesians 4:1–13, Year B). "Whoever believes and is baptized will be saved" (Mark 16:15–20, Year B). "Our bodies washed in pure water" (Hebrews 9:24–28; 10:19–23, Year C).

- *Pentecost Vigil:* "I will bring spirit into you, that you may come to life" (Ezekiel 37:1–14). "Let anyone who thirsts come to me and drink" (John 7:37–39).

- *Pentecost Sunday:* "They were all filled with the Holy Spirit" (Acts 2:1–11). "We were all baptized into one body" (1 Corinthians 12:3b–7, 12–13, Year A). "Those who belong to Christ Jesus have crucified their flesh with its passions and desires" (Galatians 5:16–25, Year B). "You received a Spirit of adoption . . . we are children of God" (Romans 8:8–17, Year C).

- *Twelfth Sunday in Ordinary Time:* "Whoever is in Christ is a new creation" (2 Corinthians 5:14–17, Year B). "All of you who were baptized into Christ have clothed yourselves with Christ" (Galatians 3:26–29, Year C). "If anyone wishes to come after me, he must . . . take up his cross daily and follow me" (Luke 9:18–24, Year C).

- *Thirteenth Sunday in Ordinary Time:* "We who were baptized into Christ Jesus were baptized into his death" (Romans 6:3–4, 8–11, Year A). "Follow me" (Luke 9:51–62, Year C).

- *Fourteenth Sunday in Ordinary Time:* "Come to me . . . and I will give you rest" (Matthew 11:25–30, Year A).

- *Fifteenth Sunday in Ordinary Time:* "He destined us for adoption to himself through Jesus Christ" (Ephesians 1:3–14, Year B).

- *Seventeenth Sunday in Ordinary Time:* "One Lord, one faith, one baptism" (Ephesians 4:1–6, Year B). "You were buried with him in baptism" (Colossians 2:12–14, Year C).

- *Eighteenth Sunday in Ordinary Time:* "Come to the water" (Isaiah 55:1–3, Year A).

- *Twenty-Second Sunday in Ordinary Time:* "Whoever wishes to come after me must deny himself, take up his cross, and follow me" (Matthew 16:21–27, Year A).

- *Twenty-Third Sunday in Ordinary Time:* "'Ephphatha!'— that is, 'Be opened!'" (Mark 7:31–37, Year B).

- *Twenty-Fourth Sunday in Ordinary Time:* "Whoever wishes to come after me must deny himself, take up his cross, and follow me" (Mark 8:27–35, Year B).

- *Twenty-Seventh Sunday in Ordinary Time:* "Let the children come to me" (Mark 10:2–16, Year B).

- *Twenty-Eighth Sunday in Ordinary Time:* "If we have died with him we shall also live with him" (2 Timothy 2:8–13, Year C).
- *Twenty-Ninth Sunday in Ordinary Time:* "I have called you by your name" (Isaiah 45:1, 4–6, Year A).
- *Thirty-Third Sunday in Ordinary Time:* "You are children of the light" (1 Thessalonians 5:1–6, Year A).
- *Our Lord Jesus Christ, King of the Universe:* "Who has made us into a kingdom, priests for his God and Father" (Revelation 1:5–8, Year B). "Who has made you fit to share in the inheritance of the holy ones in light" (Colossians 1:12–20, Year C).
- *Nativity of St. John the Baptist (when June 24 falls on a Sunday):* "The LORD called me from birth" (Isaiah 49:1–6).
- *Exaltation of the Holy Cross (when September 14 falls on a Sunday):* "Everyone who believes in him may have eternal life" (John 3:13–17).
- *All Saints (when November 1 falls on a Sunday):* "We are God's children now" (1 John 3:1–3).

While this list does not include Sundays in Advent and Lent, baptism may be celebrated during those seasons. The general rule is that "the celebration of Baptism should take place during the first weeks after the birth of the child. If there is no hope whatever that the child will be brought up in the Catholic religion, the Baptism is to be delayed."[11] Assuming that it does not interfere with this general rule, a pastor may decide not to schedule baptisms during Advent and Lent based on the principle that "it is for the pastor of the parish . . . to decide the times for the Baptism of children, keeping in mind any regulations laid down by the Conference of Bishops."[12]

Liturgical Ministries

When baptism is celebrated at Sunday Mass, not only is there an assembly of the parish community, but other liturgical ministers are also typically present to serve that assembly. If the parish has greeters or ministers of hospitality, they are at the doors of the church to welcome everyone, and they should be forewarned that a baptism will be celebrated at the Mass so that they can be attentive to visiting family members and

---

11. OBC, 8.3.
12. OBC, 8.4.

friends who may not be familiar with the church or who may not be Catholic. Remind the greeters of what the author of the Letter to the Hebrews said: "Do not neglect to show hospitality to strangers, for by doing that some have entertained angels without knowing it."[13] Presumably, servers, readers, music ministers, and, if necessary, extraordinary ministers of holy Communion would also already be scheduled if baptism were celebrated at Sunday Mass. Readers should be forewarned if a reading from the "Conferral of Infant Baptism" section of the *Lectionary for Mass* is replacing a reading for that Sunday, while the music ministers would need to plan music for the elements of the baptismal rite, including the procession after the rite of receiving the children at the door of the church, the procession to the baptistery, and the acclamation after the baptism.[14]

In addition to the usual liturgical ministries at Sunday Mass, members of a baptismal ministry at some parishes may assist with the celebration of the sacrament. This ministry could include parishioners who assist with parent preparation sessions prior to the baptism, with the baptismal liturgy, and with outreach to families after the baptism. On the day of the baptismal liturgy, members of the baptismal ministry could assist the greeters in welcoming the child's family when they arrive at the church and showing them to their seats in the church. They could assist during the celebration of baptism by handing the priest the container with the oil of catechumens for the anointing before baptism and the container of sacred chrism for the anointing after baptism, by handing the parents a towel in which to wrap their child after baptism by immersion, and by taking the paschal candle out of its stand so that a member of the family can light the child's baptismal candle. (See the list of "Additional Minister Responsibilities" in the appendix.)

Reflection Questions

1. How does the Church's emphasis on a communal celebration of baptism affirm or challenge your assumptions about celebrating this sacrament?

2. If your parish does not celebrate baptism at Sunday Mass, what fears or concerns do you need to confront about doing this?

---

13. Hebrews 13:2.
14. OBC, 42, 52, 60.

3. If your parish celebrates baptism at Sunday Mass, is there good communication with the liturgical ministers scheduled for the Mass so that they can be prepared for the baptism?

Baptism outside of Mass

When baptism is celebrated outside of Sunday Mass, it is certainly more difficult to attract an assembly that includes more than just the family and friends of the child being baptized. As deacons, our enthusiasm for presiding at the celebration of the sacrament of baptism should never get in the way of encouraging parents to celebrate the baptism of their child in the midst of an assembly of parishioners, and that will usually mean celebrating baptism at Sunday Mass where we deacons assist but do not preside. If a pastoral decision is made to celebrate baptism outside of Sunday Mass, we need to remember that it is still a liturgy of the Church that calls for a full and beautiful celebration. That includes encouraging the participation of other members of the parish and providing liturgical ministers to serve the assembly.

The first chapter in the *Order of Baptism of Children* is the "Order of Baptism for Several Children." By placing this chapter first, the Church reflects its preference for "a common celebration for all the newly born."[15] In parishes with a very small number of baptisms, it may not be unusual to use the second chapter, the "Order of Baptism for One Child," but when two or more babies are born within a few weeks of each other, a common celebration using the "Order of Baptism for Several Children" is considered to be the norm. Highlighting its preference for communal celebrations of baptism, the rite goes so far as to say that "except for a just cause, Baptism should not be celebrated twice on the same day in the same church."[16] Depending on the number of children baptized in a given year, the parish could determine the appropriate frequency for the celebration of baptism outside of Mass. The dates and times could be publicized in the parish bulletin and social media sites with an invitation for parishioners to participate.

---

15. OBC, 32.
16. CI, 27.

Liturgical Ministries in Baptisms outside of Mass

Just as some parishes have a roster of liturgical ministers who are willing to serve at funerals, so greeters, servers, readers, and music ministers could be invited to serve at baptisms that take place outside of Sunday Mass. As mentioned earlier, parishioners who serve in a baptismal ministry could also serve in these roles at the baptismal liturgy. If the parish has a paid music minister, encourage the pastor to speak with him or her about coordinating music for these baptismal liturgies and about the appropriate remuneration for this additional work. All of these ministers contribute to a fully celebrated baptismal liturgy outside of Mass.

Greeters play a particularly important role at a celebration of baptism outside of Mass. Especially when other members of the parish are not present, the greeters extend the hospitality of the local parish to the families and friends of the children to be baptized, including Catholics who may not have been to church in a while, people from various religious traditions, and people with no religious affiliation. The hospitality ministers can escort people to their seats and point out the location of restrooms and places to change the babies. When the baptismal liturgy is about to begin, the greeters can escort the parents with their children and the godparents to the door of the church and, following the rite of receiving the children at the door of the church, they can accompany them in procession to their seats for the Liturgy of the Word.

The Liturgy of the Word during the baptismal liturgy "is intended to stir up the faith of the parents and godparents and others present,"[17] and so it is important that the Scripture readings be proclaimed well by trained readers. If parish readers are not available to serve at celebrations of baptism outside of Mass, members of the parish baptismal ministry could be trained for this role. Since the Word of God is addressed especially to those who have accompanied the children to be baptized and because there is usually no time to rehearse with someone who previously has not read in church, it is usually better to invite someone other than a member of the children's families or friends to proclaim the readings. If a family member or friend who has served as a reader would like to proclaim the Scriptures at the baptismal liturgy, be sure to send the reading to this person in advance so that he or she can prepare to read.

---

17. OBC, 17.

A server trained to assist at a baptism outside of Mass can be a great help to the priest or deacon who is presiding. The server can hold the ritual book while the presider is signing the children during the rite of receiving the children, anointing the children, touching the water, and baptizing the children. The server can present the presider with the oil of catechumens and the sacred chrism, give the parents a towel in which to wrap their children after baptism by immersion, and present the parents or godparents with a candle for the handing on of a lighted candle. As with the role of greeter and reader, members of the parish baptismal ministry can be trained for this role if servers are not available to assist at baptisms outside of Mass.

The rite notes that "the celebration of Baptism is greatly enhanced by singing—to stimulate a sense of unity among those present, to foster their common prayer, and to express the paschal joy with which the rite should resound."[18] Just as music usually is included when baptism is celebrated during a Sunday Mass, music should be part of celebrations of baptism outside of Mass. Music ministers can lead the assembly in singing at the various places where the rite notes that music may be used: the beginning of the celebration, the procession from the door of the church to the place for the Liturgy of the Word, the responsorial psalm, the litany of saints, the procession to the baptistery, the profession of faith, the acclamation after the baptism, the procession to the altar, and the conclusion of the celebration.[19] No less than at weddings where a diverse assembly gathers, an effective cantor and an organist or other instrumentalist can contribute to the beauty of the celebration by leading the assembly gathered for a baptism outside of Mass to participate in the music.

Reflection Questions

1. How can parishioners be invited and encouraged to participate in baptisms that are celebrated outside of Mass?

2. If multiple celebrations of baptism outside of Mass for one child are scheduled on the same day or on consecutive Sundays, how might your parish move toward "a common celebration for all the newly born"?[20]

---

18. CI, 33.
19. OBC, 35, 42, 44, 46, 52, 59, 60, 67, 71.
20. OBC, 32.

3. If the celebration of baptism outside of Mass in your parish does not include the participation of greeters, readers, servers, and music ministers, how might you move toward enhancing these celebrations through the participation of these ministries?

Careful Use of Symbols and Ritual Gestures

The previous chapter explored the rich theological significance of the primary symbols of the baptismal liturgy: procession, water, anointing, the lighted candle. A well-prepared celebration of baptism that makes careful and beautiful use of these symbols can convey their significance, while an unprepared celebration and a minimalist use of these symbols will obscure their significance. As Pope Benedict XVI writes, "Beauty . . . is not mere decoration, but rather an essential element of the liturgical action, since it is an attribute of God himself and his revelation. These considerations should make us realize the care which is needed, if the liturgical action is to reflect its innate splendor."[21] Beauty in the liturgy does not imply extravagance, a particular style, or a particular degree of formality. Rather, we experience beauty in the liturgy when the symbols, gestures, and actions are genuine and full and when they reveal the presence and grace of God. This applies equally to celebrations of baptism within Mass and outside of Mass.

When the processions of the baptismal liturgy are approached with this understanding, the processions no longer simply function as a way to get from point A to point B but are "a religious act, a retinue of the Lord progressing through his land, so that an 'epiphany' may take place."[22] With grace and purpose, lead the parents with their children and the godparents in the processions of the baptismal liturgy: from the door of the church to the ambo, from the ambo to the baptistery, and from the baptistery to the altar. At a baptism outside of Mass, if the assembly is small, invite everyone to accompany the parents, children, and godparents in these processions.

When we baptize in water and anoint with sacred chrism, "something more is required than the mere observance of the laws governing

---

21. *Sacramentum caritatis*, 35.
22. Romano Guardini, "Open Letter to Liturgical Congress at Mainz," *Herder Correspondence* 1, no. 1 (1964): 24.

valid and lawful celebration."[23] A few drops of water and a simple smudge of chrism meet the requirements of validity and may be all that is possible in certain extraordinary situations, but a celebration of baptism in the ordinary environment of a parish church calls for "outward forms meant to evoke and emphasize the grandeur of the event being celebrated."[24] Use a generous amount of water and encourage the practice of baptism by immersion. Pour enough chrism on the crown of each child's head and gently rub the chrism into each child's head so that "the anointing with this oil causes our (may cause the children's) faces to be joyful and serene" and so that "those formed into a temple of your [God's] majesty by the holiness infused through this anointing and by the cleansing of the stain of their first birth / be made fragrant with the innocence of a life pleasing to you."[25]

The clothing with a white garment and the handing on of a lighted candle are two of the explanatory rites that take place after the anointing with sacred chrism. While minor in comparison to the baptism in water and anointing with sacred chrism, these rites also need to be celebrated with beauty and integrity. Whether baptism is celebrated by immersion or by pouring water over the child's head, let the clothing with a white garment be genuine by placing the baptismal garment on the child *after* the baptism. Only when the child is dressed in the baptismal garment *after* the baptism does the accompanying text make sense: "You have become a new creation / and have clothed yourselves in Christ."[26] Ask the parents to bring the child to church in other clothes, and then give the parents time to dress the child in the baptismal garment after the baptism. Avoid the practice of placing a bib or other cloth over the baptismal garment and pretending that it is the baptismal garment. For the handing on of a lighted candle, recall the suggestions offered in the previous chapter about using a paschal candle and a baptismal candle whose size and beauty can convey the image of the light of Christ. "The living flame of the candle, symbolic of the risen Christ, reminds people that in baptism they are brought out of darkness into God's marvelous light."[27]

---

23. CSL, 11.
24. Pope John Paul II, *Ecclesia de Eucharistia*, 49.
25. *Order of Blessing the Oil of Catechumens and of the Sick and of Consecrating the Chrism*, 25.1.
26. OBC, 63.
27. BLS, 92.

"The beauty of the Liturgy is manifested concretely through material objects and bodily gestures,"[28] and so the ritual gestures made during the celebration of baptism are an important consideration. The priest or deacon who is presiding can provide a good model for this in the way he carries out the ritual gestures that are unique to his role. Primary among these are the gestures associated with baptizing and anointing. Take time to practice the gestures associated with immersing a child, pouring water over a child's head, and anointing a child on the crown of the head with chrism. Become familiar enough with the rite that you can look up and into the eyes of the parents, the child, the godparents, and the assembly when addressing them. Process from one station of the baptismal liturgy to the next with grace and in a way that is not rushed. Position yourself during the different parts of the rite so that you are not impeding the assembly's ability to see what is going on. Proclaim the texts of the rite clearly and at a moderate pace. Take to heart the wise advice Father Robert Hovda offered several decades ago: "Few things threaten one's effectiveness as a presider and the presence one has to establish as much as the lust for efficiency. . . . Better use one gesture and make it a real picture, make it big and broad and smooth, than try to signify anything with a hundred muscular spasms. Do not hurry. Do not abbreviate. Do not shortchange. Do not condense. Do not telescope. Do not 'reduce to essentials' in the sense of 'getting everything in' no matter what the cost or speed."[29]

Reflection Questions

1. Think about the way that symbols are used in the celebration of baptism in your parish. Does it reflect care and beauty? Is it able to convey the presence and grace of God?

2. If possible, ask someone to make a video of a celebration of baptism at which you preside. As you watch the video, are there aspects of your presiding style or the way that you carry out the ritual gestures of the baptismal rite that you want to change?

28. Office for the Liturgical Celebrations of the Supreme Pontiff, "Beauty in Every Aspect of the Liturgical Rite."
29. Robert W. Hovda, *Strong, Loving and Wise* (Washington, DC: The Liturgical Conference, 1976), 58.

Chapter 4

The Deacon's Role in the Rite

Prior to the Second Vatican Council, the rite used for the baptism of children was an adaptation of the rite for the baptism of adults. In the *Constitution on the Sacred Liturgy* in 1963, the Second Vatican Council called for the revision of the rite of baptism of children and noted that "it should be suited to the fact that those to be baptized are infants."[1] The *Rite of Baptism for Children* was the first baptismal liturgy in the history of the Catholic Church that was specifically designed for infants and young children, and it was used in the United States for fifty years, from 1970 through early 2020. In early 2020, the revised *Order of Baptism of Children* was introduced in the United States, while the Spanish version, *Ritual para el Bautismo de los Niños*, was introduced in 2008. Both of these are approved translations of the Latin text *Ordo Baptismi parvulorum, editio typica altera*. In addition to a revised English translation of the Latin text of the rite, the *Order of Baptism of Children* incorporates a few adaptations that the bishops of the United States approved.

Overview of the Rite

Like all rites of the Church, the *Order of Baptism of Children* starts with an introduction. In fact, there are two introductions: the first is a thirty-five-paragraph general introduction to all of the sacraments of Christian initiation, and the second is a thirty-one-paragraph particular introduction to the baptism of children. While it may be tempting to skip these introductions and proceed directly to the texts and rubrics for baptism, the introductions present important principles for catechesis, liturgical celebration, and other aspects of pastoral practice. If you have

---

1. CSL, 67.

not read these introductions in a while or if you have never read them, take the time to do so. The introductions address the following:

- General Introduction: dignity of baptism, duties and ministries in the celebration of baptism, requisites for the celebration of baptism, adaptations within the competence of the conferences of bishops, adaptations within the competence of the minister

- Introduction to the *Order of Baptism of Children*: importance of the baptism of children, ministries and duties in the celebration of baptism, time and place for the baptism of children, structure of the rite of baptizing children, adaptations that conferences of bishops or bishops may make, adaptations within the competence of the minister

After the introductions, the first three chapters in the *Order of Baptism of Children* present three variations for the celebration of baptism:

- Chapter 1: Order of Baptism for Several Children (paragraphs 32–71)

- Chapter 2: Order of Baptism for One Child (paragraphs 72–106)

- Chapter 3: Order of Baptism for a Large Number of Children (paragraphs 107–131)

The Order of Baptism for Several Children is placed first since the norm presented in the general introduction is "a common celebration of Baptism on the same day for all newborn babies."[2] The rite does not provide specific guidance on what constitutes "several children" and what constitutes "a large number of children" and, correspondingly, on when to use chapter 1 or chapter 3. If you are accustomed to presiding or assisting at baptism for one child, then anything more than one child may seem like "a large number of children," but there are parishes where using the Order of Baptism for Several Children for six or even twelve children is not uncommon. My first job in ministry was at such a parish, and these celebrations, which took place within Mass, were well prepared, engaging, and memorable.

Chapter 4 (paragraphs 132–156), the Order of Baptism to Be Used by Catechists in the Absence of a Priest or Deacon, provides a slightly abbreviated rite of baptism that may be led by "a catechist or another person designated for this function by the local ordinary"[3] when a priest or deacon is not available. While many deacons serve in places where a priest or deacon is regularly available to preside at baptism

---

2. CI, 27.
3. *Code of Canon Law* (CIC), 861.2.

within a reasonable amount of time after the birth of a child, some deacons serve in areas where that is not the case. "These situations are common in mission territories as well as in areas of this country which suffer from a scarcity of priests and deacons."[4] While a deacon would not use chapter 4 when presiding at a baptism, he might be in a pastoral setting where he is asked to train catechists or other people designated by the bishop to lead the celebration of baptism using this chapter.

With one exception, the title of chapter 5 (paragraphs 157–164) is self-explanatory: Order of Baptism of Children in Danger of Death, or at the Point of Death, to Be Used in the Absence of a Priest or Deacon. The exception is that a priest or deacon may also use this chapter when a child is in imminent danger of death.[5] This abbreviated version of the rite includes a prayer of the faithful, a profession of faith, the baptism with the appropriate words, the clothing with a white garment, and the Lord's Prayer. At the point of death, the baptism with the appropriate words may be used without any of the other elements. Deacons who serve in hospital settings should be familiar with this chapter and should offer training for those who may be called on to be the minister of baptism when a child is in danger of death. Examples of those who may be called on include physicians, midwives, nurses, and other health-care professionals, as well as extraordinary ministers of holy Communion and ministers to the sick who serve in hospitals.

Chapter 6 (paragraphs 165–185), the Order of Bringing a Baptized Child to the Church, is used to welcome a child who was baptized outside of a church and to celebrate the parts of the baptismal liturgy that were omitted when the child was baptized. This ritual is intended primarily for a child who was baptized in danger of death using the abbreviated form of the rite in chapter 5. It may also be adapted and used for children who were baptized during "other difficulties (for example, persecution, disagreement between the parents, etc.), which prohibited the celebration of Baptism in church."[6] This chapter includes a rite of receiving the child at the door of the church, a celebration of the Word of God, a prayer of the faithful, the anointing after baptism, the clothing with a white garment, the handing on of a lighted candle, the Lord's Prayer, and a blessing and dismissal. While this chapter

---

4. Kevin T. Hart in *New Commentary on the Code of Canon Law* (Mahwah, NJ: Paulist Press, 2000), 1050.
5. See OBC, 22.
6. OBC, 185.

provides a complete outline for a celebration outside of Mass, it may also be adapted and celebrated within Mass so that the baptized child may be welcomed by a larger gathering of the parish community. This would be especially appropriate if the parish had been praying for the child's return to health in the universal prayer at Sunday Mass.

Chapter 7 (paragraphs 186–249) provides "Various Texts for Use in the Celebration of Baptism for Children." These include the Scripture readings from the "Conferral of Infant Baptism" section of the *Lectionary for Mass*, formulas for the prayer of the faithful, alternative versions of the litany of saints, the prayer of exorcism, the blessing of water and invocation of God over the water, and the final blessing, and texts for the acclamations, hymns, and chants that may be used during the baptismal liturgy.

The appendix (paragraphs 250–331), which is new to the *Order of Baptism of Children*, provides specific directions for celebrating the baptism of children within Mass. This section clarifies adaptations for integrating the celebration of baptism into Mass, such as the omission of the greeting and the penitential act during the Introductory Rites,[7] the replacement of the creed with the profession of faith before the baptism,[8] and the place of the universal prayer after the homily and before the litany of saints, prayer of exorcism, and anointing before baptism.[9] The appendix contains an introduction followed by an outline of the rite and then the text and rubrics for the Order of Baptism for Several Children within Mass and then the Order of Baptism for One Child within Mass.

Reflection Questions

1. Spend some time looking through the *Order of Baptism of Children*. Have you read the two introductions to the rite? Are there ways in which the introductions enhance your understanding of the baptism of children?

2. Are you familiar with the Order of Baptism of Children in Danger of Death in chapter 5? Is training for this version of the rite available in your area for physicians, midwives, nurses, and other health-care

---

7. OBC, 251.1.
8. OBC, 251.3.
9. OBC, 272, 310.

professionals, as well as extraordinary ministers of holy Communion and ministers to the sick who serve in hospitals?

The Deacon Assisting in a Celebration of Baptism within Mass

When baptism is celebrated within Mass, there are some variations in the deacon's usual role at Mass. While the priest who presides at Mass also typically presides at the celebration of baptism within the Mass, there are ways in which the deacon assists during the celebration of baptism.

Introductory Rites: The deacon accompanies the priest to the door of the church for the rite of receiving the children. As the parents respond to the priest's questions at the door of the church, the deacon or another assistant minister could hold a microphone for the parents so that all in the assembly may hear their responses. The deacon accompanies the priest from the door of the church to the sanctuary, where they bow and kiss the altar. If the deacon announces the invocations in the third form of the penitential act, he will not do so since the penitential act is omitted.

Liturgy of the Word: When baptism is celebrated at a Sunday Mass, the norm is that "the readings are taken from the Mass of the day," but the rite also gives the option of choosing one or more readings from the "Conferral of Infant Baptism" section of the *Lectionary for Mass* during Christmas Time and Ordinary Time, as well as when baptism is celebrated within a weekday Mass.[10] The deacon should confirm with the priest which Gospel reading he will proclaim at the Mass. Only one Gospel reading from the "Conferral of Infant Baptism" section of the *Lectionary for Mass* appears in the *Book of the Gospels* (Mark 12:28b–34, see Thirty-First Sunday in Ordinary Time, Year B), so if the priest has chosen a Gospel passage that does not appear in the *Book of the Gospels*, the deacon should be prepared to proclaim the Gospel from the *Lectionary for Mass* instead. If the deacon reads the intercessions of the universal prayer, he needs to be ready to do this after the period of silent reflection that follows the homily since the creed is replaced by the profession of faith that takes place before the baptism.

---

10. OBC, 269, 307.

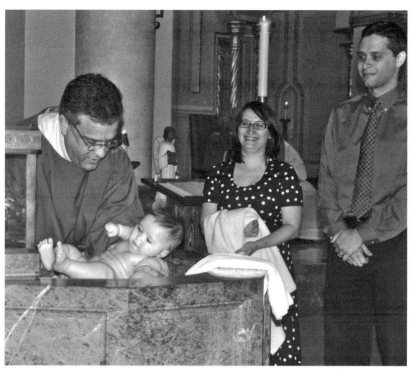

The generous use of water in baptism by immersion is a fuller sign of the child entering into the paschal mystery. During a celebration of baptism of several children, the deacon may baptize some of the children.

Celebration of Baptism: Since the priest who presides at Mass is typically the minister for a baptism within that Mass, there is no specific role for the deacon in the celebration of baptism for one child within Mass. In the absence of other assistant ministers, however, the deacon can certainly assist by handing the priest the vessel with the oil of catechumens for the anointing before baptism and the vessel with the sacred chrism for the anointing after baptism, handing the parents a towel in which to wrap the child after baptism by immersion, and holding the paschal candle so that the parents can light the baptismal candles. In the celebration of baptism for several children, the rite notes that the priest and the deacon may each anoint some of the children before baptism, may each baptize some of the children, and may each anoint some of the children after baptism.[11]

---

11. OBC, 275, 286, 287.

Liturgy of the Eucharist: The deacon's role in the Liturgy of the Eucharist is the same as at any Sunday Mass.

Concluding Rites: The *Order of Baptism of Children* provides formulas for the final blessing, and if one of these is used, the deacon invites the assembly to "bow down for the blessing." The deacon proclaims the dismissal as usual.

Reflection Questions

1. Think about the celebration of baptism within Mass at your parish. Are there members of a baptismal ministry or other parishioners who assist with important details such as welcoming the families of the children and showing them to their seats in the church; accompanying the parents, godparents, and children to the door of the church for the start of the liturgy; holding a microphone for the parents as they make their responses at the door of the church; handing the parents a towel in which to wrap the children after baptism by immersion; and holding the paschal candle so that the parents can light the baptismal candles? In the absence of such assistants, how might you assist with such things?

2. Do you and the priest have a good understanding of your respective roles in the celebration of baptism within Mass? Have you walked through the details of the rite together in the church so that each of you knows who does what and when?

The Deacon Presiding in a Celebration of Baptism outside of Mass

When baptism is celebrated outside of Mass, it is increasingly common for deacons to preside at the celebration, and most deacons enthusiastically embrace this role. As deacons review their role as presiders in the *Order of Baptism of Children*, it is important to recall what was said in previous chapters, including the Church's preference for "a common celebration of Baptism on the same day for all newborn babies,"[12] the participation of "the People of God— represented not only by godparents, parents, and relatives, but also, insofar as possible, by friends, acquaintances,

---

12. CI, 27.

neighbors, and some members of the local Church,"[13] the service of various liturgical ministers, and honoring the meaning of the sacrament through the full use of symbols and gestures.

Choice of Rite

In small parishes with few baptisms, deacons may use the Order of Baptism for One Child most commonly. In places where two or more children are presented for baptism in the same period of time, a common celebration using the Order of Baptism for Several Children is typically the appropriate choice. The major difference between the Order of Baptism for Several Children and the Order of Baptism for a Large Number of Children is the omission of the anointing with the oil of catechumens and of the "ephphatha" rite in the Order of Baptism for a Large Number of Children, but the Order of Baptism for Several Children offers the option of omitting these also.[14] Since the Order of Baptism for Several Children and the Order of Baptism for a Large Number of Children are not all that different in their liturgical structure, the more important issue is how the deacon prepares for and leads a beautiful and engaging celebration of baptism for multiple children.

Some deacons, as well as some families and parishioners, shy away from baptisms involving more than one child because of negative experiences with baptisms of multiple children. The problem is not so much with the rite or the baptism of multiple children in the same celebration as it is with a lack of attention to the demands of the rite. The architect Mies van der Rohe was fond of saying, "God is in the details," and liturgical documents note that the various elements of a liturgy "must be conducive to making the entire celebration resplendent with beauty and noble simplicity, to making clear the true and full meaning of its different parts, and to fostering the participation of all."[15] When the deacon is presiding at a baptism for multiple children, he needs to focus on leading a larger assembly in prayer, and that requires a different level of energy than in a smaller celebration for one child. It also requires the assistance of ministers who can attend to the other details of the rite, for example, graciously welcoming the parents and godparents and prompting them when it is time to move, holding the

---

13. CI, 7.
14. OBC, 51, 65.
15. *General Instruction of the Roman Missal* (GIRM), 42.

microphone for the parents as they make their responses at the door
of the church, handing the oil of catechumens and the sacred chrism
to the deacon when they are needed, offering towels to the parents so
that they can wrap their children after baptism by immersion, handing
the baptismal candles to the parents, holding the paschal candle as the
parents light the baptismal candles, proclaiming the Scripture readings,
and leading the assembly in song. (See the more complete checklist of
"assistant minister responsibilities" in the appendix of this book.) When
a celebration of baptism for multiple children has the assistance of other
ministers who unobtrusively attend to these details, along with effective
presiding by the deacon, the assembly experiences the difference that
the bishops of the United States describe: "Faith grows when it is well
expressed in celebration. Good celebrations can foster and nourish faith.
Poor celebrations may weaken it."[16]

As we turn now to a review of the four parts of the celebration of
baptism outside of Mass, we will refer primarily to the Order of Baptism
for Several Children, while noting any differences for the baptism of one
child or a large number of children.

Rite of Receiving the Children

The vesture for a deacon who presides at a celebration of baptism outside
of Mass is "an alb or surplice and stole, and even a cope, in a festive
color."[17] The deacon does not wear a dalmatic in this situation. When the
baptismal liturgy is ready to begin, the deacon "goes with the ministers
to the door of the church, or to that part of the church where the parents
and godparents are gathered with those to be baptized."[18] While the rite
mentions the option of gathering in another part of the church, the norm
is that the baptismal liturgy begin at the door of the church since the
children are "literally 'entering the church,' and crossing this threshold
represents entering the community's embrace."[19] Ideally, a greeter, a
member of the baptismal ministry, or another assistant minister has
greeted the families as they arrived at the church, shown them to their
seats, and then led the parents, children, and godparents to the door
of the church a few minutes before the start of the liturgy. At the door

---

16. *Sing to the Lord: Music in Divine Worship* (STL), 5.
17. OBC, 35.
18. OBC, 35.
19. Paul Turner, *Your Child's Baptism* (Chicago: LTP, 2018), 19.

of the church, the deacon greets all who have gathered. The rite provides a sample text for this greeting but also notes that the deacon may use "these or similar words."[20] As the first words of the baptismal liturgy, this greeting should be proclaimed in a strong, clear, and inviting tone of voice, using a microphone unless the assembly is quite small and all have gathered in close proximity at the church door along with the parents, children, and godparents.

After the greeting, the deacon asks the parents four questions. He begins with the queries "What name do you give (or have you given) your child?" and "What do you ask of God's Church for N.?" When there is more than one child to be baptized, the deacon asks these questions to each set of parents. The rite notes, however, that the questions may be posed to all of the parents at once "if there are many to be baptized."[21] In this case, each set of parents would reply to the first question in turn, while all the parents would join in responding, "Baptism," to the second question at the same time. In the Order of Baptism for a Large Number of Children, the first question is omitted. The deacon then summarizes the parents' responsibility to raise their children in the faith and asks them, "Do you understand this responsibility?" The response, "We do," is given by each set of parents or, if there are many children to be baptized, the response may be given by all of the parents at the same time. If the parents respond individually to the questions, using a microphone will help the assembly hear the parents' responses. An assistant minister can hold the microphone for each set of parents. It can be awkward when all hear the question the deacon poses but not the parents' response. In the last of the four questions, the deacon asks the godparents, "Are you ready to help the parents of these children in their duty?" Together, the godparents respond, "We are."

The deacon's next line is one of the only places in the rite in which the children are addressed directly. Since the Church understands that the children "cannot profess the faith for themselves . . . [and that] they are baptized in the faith of the Church . . . which is proclaimed by the parents and godparents and the others present,"[22] the questions in the rite are addressed to the parents and the godparents. The deacon's line here does not expect a response from the children, but instead announces

20. OBC, 36.
21. OBC, 38.
22. OBC, 1–2.

After the readings, the deacon preaches a brief homily so that those present may grasp the deeper meaning and responsibilities of baptism.

that "the Church of God receives you with great joy."[23] Then, the deacon makes the sign of the cross on the forehead of each child and invites the parents and the godparents to make the sign of the cross on the forehead of their children. Similar to the signing with the cross in the rite of acceptance into the order of catechumens,[24] the signing of the children "marks with the imprint of Christ the one who is going to belong to him and signifies the grace of the redemption Christ won for us by his cross."[25] The deacon should honor the meaning of this gesture by drawing the cross on the forehead of each child slowly and deliberately, not hastily drawing the cross in the air above the forehead. Only in a celebration involving a large number of children would the deacon make the sign of the cross over all the children at once.[26]

23. OBC, 41.
24. *Rite of Christian Initiation of Adults*, 54–57.
25. CCC, 1235.
26. OBC, 111.

The first of the processions of the baptismal liturgy moves the deacon, parents, godparents, and children from the door of the church to their places for the Liturgy of the Word, preferably with singing to accompany the procession. Although the rite does not exclude other options for singing, the short section of Psalm 85 that is suggested[27] makes it clear that this music is intended to accompany the procession and is not intended to continue after the procession ends.

Sacred Celebration of the Word of God

"Sacred Scripture is of the greatest importance in the celebration of the liturgy,"[28] and the celebration of baptism outside of Mass is no exception. To emphasize how important the Liturgy of the Word is for the parents and godparents, the rite notes that "while the Liturgy of the Word is celebrated, it is desirable that children should be taken to a separate place. But care should be taken that the parents and godparents attend the Liturgy of the Word; the children should therefore be entrusted to the care of others."[29] This allows the parents and godparents to focus on the Liturgy of the Word without distraction, and it avoids the temptation to rush through the celebration of the Word of God if the children get fussy or cry. During a prebaptismal meeting, parents can be invited to line up a family member or friend to take their child to a separate place, if needed, during the celebration of baptism. This separate place should be clean, comfortable, easily accessible, equipped with a place to feed and change the children if needed and, if possible, a television or other monitor to allow the people who accompany the children to see and hear the Liturgy of the Word. A member of the baptismal ministry or another assistant minister can lead these people and the children to the place at the appropriate time.

The rite indicates that one or two readings from the "Conferral of Infant Baptism" section of the *Lectionary for Mass* should be read, although it also notes that other Scripture readings "suited to the wishes or needs of the parents"[30] may be used. If, for example, parents mention a particular Scripture passage during a prebaptismal meeting, and if that reading speaks of baptism or some aspect of the life of Christian

27. OBC, 42.
28. CSL, 24.
29. OBC, 14.
30. OBC, 44.

discipleship, the deacon could affirm and encourage the parents' love of Scripture by using and preaching on that reading during the celebration of baptism. While a Gospel reading is proclaimed by the deacon, any other Scripture readings should be proclaimed by other ministers, such as a parish reader or a member of the baptismal ministry. A responsorial psalm, preferably sung and led by a cantor, could be used between the readings.

After the readings, the deacon "preaches a brief homily in which light is shed on what has been read, and those present are led to a deeper understanding of the mystery of Baptism and to a more eager fulfillment of the responsibility that arises from it, especially for parents and godparents."[31] This rubric provides two important reminders about the homily in a celebration of baptism: it should not be omitted, and it should be brief. President Franklin Roosevelt advised public speakers to "be sincere, be brief, and be seated," and Monsignor James Mongelluzzo, who teaches liturgy and homiletics at Pope Saint John XXIII National Seminary, has adapted Roosevelt's advice as a teaching point for homilists: "Be clear, be brief, and be seated." Crafting a clear and brief homily for the celebration of baptism takes time and preparation. The following are issues to consider from the wisdom provided in several homiletics resources:

- In their document on preaching, *Fulfilled in Your Hearing*, the Bishops' Committee on Priestly Life and Ministry began by focusing the homilist's attention on the assembly and noted that "the diversity of every assembly is a factor that needs to be taken seriously by the preacher."[32] At a celebration of baptism, this assembly includes not only the parents and godparents but also a diverse mix of family members and friends. Father James Wallace, CSSR, notes that the goal of the homilist in this situation is to "touch the hearts of the congregation so that they can enter prayerfully into the subsequent ritual and go on to live in a way that supports this event in their daily lives. . . . The question is: how does this text bring meaning to the event that is being celebrated by this community today?"[33]

- Father Robert Waznak, PSS, reminds homilists that the homily at a celebration of baptism "should be designed to do what any homily is

---

31. OBC, 45.
32. Bishops' Committee on Priestly Life and Ministry, *Fulfilled in Your Hearing: The Homily in the Sunday Assembly*, 9.
33. James A. Wallace, CSSR, "Preaching, Special Occasions," in *The New Dictionary of Sacramental Worship* (Collegeville, MN: Liturgical Press, 1990), 994.

supposed to do: give thanks and praise to God, especially for what God has done for us in the paschal mystery of Christ and continues to do in the Holy Spirit."[34] Based on the guideline that the homily "should be an explanation of some aspect of the readings from Sacred Scripture or of another text from the Ordinary or the Proper of the Mass of the day,"[35] Father Waznak encourages homilists at ritual celebrations such as baptism to "pay attention not only to the biblical texts but to the prayers, actions, and rhythm of the rite itself."[36]

- Affirming that "the meaning of baptism is best seen through the ceremonies by which it is celebrated,"[37] Father Alfred McBride, OPRAEM, directs homilists to the various elements of the baptismal liturgy to discover more about the mystery of baptism. He connects these to various catechetical points about baptism that could be included in the homily.

- Father Raúl Gómez, SDS, reviews principles and characteristics of Hispanic culture and spirituality that a homilist needs to keep in mind when preaching at ritual celebrations such as baptism "among Latinos, for those occasions are key events that lift up and celebrate Hispanic culture, identity, and sacramentality. For effective preaching, the preacher must connect Latinos to their religious experience, must know who the audience is and what will help the hearers make this connection. The preacher must have a keen understanding of where, how, and when Latinos encounter God in their lives."[38]

As at any liturgy, times of silence during the celebration of baptism are "part of the celebration . . . [and] after the Homily, all meditate briefly on what they have heard."[39] Following this period of silence, the deacon introduces the prayer of the faithful. The rite offers five sets of intercessions but notes that other intercessions may be used "so that the prayer may be more suitable, and most importantly take account of the special needs of the families."[40] Since the deacon is presiding and introduces the prayer of the faithful, it is more appropriate for someone other than the deacon to read the intercessions. The rite indicates that a reader does this, but it could also be a member of the baptismal ministry

---

34. Robert P. Waznak, PSS, *An Introduction to the Homily* (Collegeville, MN: Liturgical Press, 1998), 115.
35. GIRM, 65.
36. Waznak, *An Introduction to the Homily*, 116.
37. Alfred McBride, OPRAEM, *How to Make Homilies Better, Briefer, and Bolder* (Huntington, IN: Our Sunday Visitor Publishing Division, 2007), 106.
38. Raúl Gómez, SDS, "Preaching the Ritual Masses among Latinos," in Preaching and Culture in Latino Congregations, ed. Kenneth G. Davis and Jorge L. Presmanes (Chicago: LTP, 2000), 119.
39. GIRM, 45.
40. OBC, chapter 7, II. Formulas for the Prayer of the Faithful.

or another assistant minister if a parish reader is not present. The prayer of the faithful ends not with a concluding prayer as at Mass, but with a litany of saints to which may be added the "Patron Saints of the children or of the church or of the place."[41] Children who were taken to a separate place for the Liturgy of the Word are brought back into the church before the litany of saints begins.

This part of the baptismal liturgy ends with the prayer of exorcism and anointing before baptism. The oil of catechumens is used for this anointing, which is done on the breast of the children. During a prebaptismal meeting, the parents should be told that they will need to loosen their children's clothing so that the deacon can anoint the children on their breast. The rite indicates that "in the United States, if, for serious reasons, the celebrant judges it pastorally necessary or desirable, the Anointing before Baptism may be omitted."[42] In the Order of Baptism for a Large Number of Children, this anointing is omitted "because of the number to be baptized."[43] When this anointing is omitted, the prayer to introduce the anointing is adapted to omit the reference to the anointing, and the deacon lays his hand on each of the children instead.

The transition from the Liturgy of the Word to the celebration of baptism is marked by the second procession of the baptismal liturgy. If the baptismal font is located in a separate baptistery or a part of the church that is not visible to the assembly, all may join in the procession to this place. If the baptismal font is visible to the assembly, the deacon, parents, and godparents process to the font with the children. As with the procession from the door of the church earlier in the celebration, the rite encourages singing during the procession to the baptismal font. Psalm 23 is offered as a suggestion for this song.

Celebration of Baptism

The next part of the baptismal liturgy begins with the blessing of water and invocation of God over the water. Using the first option for the text of this prayer, we explored the prayer's rich theological themes in chapter 2. There are, however, two additional options for this prayer in chapter 7 of the rite. One of these options should be used "during Easter Time . . . if the baptismal water has been consecrated at the Easter Vigil, so that

---

41. OBC, 48.
42. OBC, 51.
43. OBC, 115.

the Baptism may not lack the element of thanksgiving and petition."[44] In other words, the blessing is not repeated if the baptism is celebrated during Easter Time (Easter Sunday through Pentecost Sunday) and the water used for baptism was already blessed at the Easter Vigil. A prayer of thanksgiving and petition is still used. When one of these two prayers is used during Easter Time with water that was blessed at the Easter Vigil, the section marked by an asterisk is omitted and replaced by the single paragraph that begins "By the mystery of this blessed water."[45]

The format of these two additional prayers is also different in that the assembly makes a response at the end of each paragraph of the prayer. Most people will not be familiar with this response and will need some type of cue to respond. A worship aid with this response and other texts for the assembly could be distributed to each person at the beginning of the celebration, although a more effective approach might be for a cantor to sing the response and then lead the assembly in repeating it at the end of each paragraph.[46] In two of the three options for this prayer,[47] the deacon touches the water with his right hand as he proclaims the final paragraph of the prayer, while in the third option,[48] he makes the sign of the cross over the water as he begins the final paragraph. Like all gestures in the liturgy, these gestures should be made gracefully and with purpose.

Since children "are baptized in the faith of the Church herself, which is proclaimed by the parents and godparents and the others present,"[49] the deacon leads the parents and godparents in the renunciation of sin and the profession of faith just before the baptism in water. This begins with a brief address to the parents and godparents. The deacon should develop enough familiarity with this address that he is able to look up at the parents and godparents at least occasionally rather than keeping his head focused on the ritual book throughout the address. There are two options for the renunciation of sin. The parents and godparents respond, "I do," to each of the three questions for the renunciation of sin and to each of the three questions for the profession of

---

44. OBC, 55.
45. OBC, 223–24.
46. See, for example, Lourdes Montgomery's bilingual composition "Blessing of Water/Bendición del Agua Bautismal" (OCP Publications, 2004): "Springs of water, bless the Lord. Give him glory and praise for ever. / Fuentes del Señor, bendigan al Señor, glorifíquenlo y alábenlo."
47. OBC, 54, 223.
48. OBC, 224.
49. OBC, 2.

faith. The rest of the assembly "gives assent to this profession of faith"[50]
by saying, "Amen," after the deacon says, "This is our faith. This is the
faith of the Church. We are proud to profess it in Christ Jesus our Lord."
In some parishes, the entire assembly is invited to join the parents and
godparents in responding, "I do," to the questions for the renunciation
of sin and the profession of faith. This adaptation seems appropriate
given the indication in the rite that "the profession of faith . . . is made
by the entire community before the Baptism."[51]

Immediately before the baptism, the deacon asks the parents and
godparents, "Is it your will, therefore, that N. should receive Baptism
in the faith of the Church, which we have all professed with you?" This
question is put to each set of parents and godparents, even when a large
number of children are to be baptized. After each set of parents and
godparents responds to the question, the deacon baptizes their child,
saying, "I baptize you in the name of the Father, and of the Son, and of
the Holy Spirit." The rite notes that the deacon "immerses the child or
pours water over him (her)"[52] three times. That immersion is listed as the
first of the two options for baptizing echoes the principle that immersion
"more suitably signifies participation in the Death and Resurrection
of Christ."[53] What the bishops of the United States said of immersion
regarding the Christian initiation of adults is equally true in the baptism
of children: "Baptism by immersion is the fuller and more expressive
sign of the sacrament and, therefore, is preferred. Although it is not yet
a common practice in the United States, provision should be made for
its more frequent use."[54]

Christians were originally baptized by immersion, our brothers
and sisters in the Orthodox Church have continued baptizing by immersion for centuries, and baptism by immersion has once again become a
common practice in some Roman Catholic communities. There are unique
details involved in baptism by immersion, but they are not overwhelming,
even when several children are baptized in the same celebration. During
a prebaptismal meeting, tell the parents to bring their child to the church
in clothing that is not the baptismal garment. Ask them to loosen the
child's clothing for the anointing with the oil of catechumens before the

---

50. OBC, 59.
51. OBC, 29.2.c.
52. OBC, 60.
53. CI, 22.
54. *National Statutes for the Catechumenate*, 17.

baptism and then to remove the clothing (including the diaper) and wrap the child in a blanket or towel just before the baptism. When it is time for the baptism, the parents unwrap the blanket or towel and hand the naked child to the deacon, who immerses the child three times in the font. Each deacon will need to develop his own practice for this, but it is usually best to place one hand on the back of the child's neck and the other hand on the back of the child's thighs while lowering the child into the font. By immersion, we mean that the child's body goes into the water. (We do not baptize children by submersion in which the child's head goes under the water.) After the third immersion, the deacon hands the child back to the parents, who wrap the child in a bath towel. The towel can be handed to the parents by a godparent, a member of the baptismal ministry, a server, or another assistant minister. The parents can provide the towels or the parish can maintain a supply of bath towels that are used for the celebration of baptism. If we believe what we say about baptism, then we will put the effort into working out the details of this more profound expression of baptism.

> For centuries we have for the sake of convenience been practicing baptism by pouring, with the result that the sacrament of baptism has been understood for the most part merely in terms of a kind of moral or legal purification. Yet it is clear from the teaching of the New Testament and of the Church, from the practice of the classical liturgies and from what we have seen of our own rite, that what is involved is nothing less than a transformation of the whole person so radical that it has to be described in terms of death and rebirth. This is only adequately expressed when those being baptized are really plunged into the water.[55]

The rite indicates that the assembly sings an acclamation after each baptism, and several options are given for this acclamation.[56] The acclamation that was sung during the blessing of water and invocation of God over the water could be reprised for the acclamation after baptism. Various publishers provide musical acclamations that are appropriate for this part of the rite.[57] When several children are baptized in the same

---

55. Mark Searle, *Christening: The Making of Christians* (Collegeville, MN: Liturgical Press, 1980), 88–89.
56. OBC, 60.
57. See, for example, Christopher Walker, ed., "Christ We Proclaim" (Portland: OCP Publications, 2001), 276–77.

celebration, the parents and godparents whose child has just been baptized step to the side and the next set of parents and godparents come to the font with their child as this acclamation is sung.

After the baptism in water, there is a series of four "explanatory rites": anointing after baptism, clothing with a white garment, handing on of a lighted candle, and "ephphatha." The first three take place even if a large number of children are being baptized. The "ephphatha" is omitted if a large number of children are being baptized and may be omitted at the discretion of the deacon if one child or several children are being baptized.[58] The rite assumes that these explanatory rites take place where baptism was celebrated, whether that was in a baptistery or in or near the sanctuary. If the celebration involves several children, an assistant minister could help to line up the parents, godparents, and children after each baptism so that they are visible to the assembly for the explanatory rites and so that the deacon can go to the children easily for the anointing after baptism. The texts that accompany the explanatory rites are brief and are addressed to either the children or the parents and godparents. The deacon should develop enough familiarity with these texts that he is able to look up at the children or at the parents and godparents at least occasionally as he proclaims the texts.

For the anointing after baptism, the deacon says the text once, whether there is one child or several children. Then, he "anoints each baptized child with sacred Chrism on the crown of his (her) head."[59] This is not the same as tracing the sign of the cross on the child's forehead. How can the deacon do this in such a way that the anointing can convey its rich symbolism? To suggest one option, an assistant minister begins by handing the container with the sacred chrism to the deacon, and the deacon hands the ritual book to the assistant minister. With each child lying in the arms of one of his or her parents, the deacon holds the container of chrism in one of his hands and places his other hand on the back of the child's head. The deacon slowly and visibly pours a small amount of the sacred chrism from the container onto the crown of the child's head. As the chrism reaches the child's head, the deacon uses the hand behind the child's head to rub the chrism gently into the crown of the child's head. The deacon moves to the next child and does the same. Chrism rubbed into the child's head will be absorbed

---

58. OBC, 65, 101.
59. OBC, 62.

into the hair and skin and not drip onto the child's face or neck. The child will exude the aroma of the chrism throughout the day of the baptism. There is no reason to wipe off the chrism with a towel, and to do so would minimize or even contradict the importance of this liturgical action. After anointing the children, the deacon can hand the container of chrism back to an assistant minister, wipe the excess chrism from his hand with a small towel, and receive the ritual book back from the assistant minister.

After the deacon says the text for the clothing with a white garment, the rite indicates that "a white garment is placed on each child."[60] There is a difference between placing a garment on a child and dressing a child in a garment. Since dressing the children in the white garments will likely take more time than the rite anticipates at this point, the garment can simply be placed on the children at this time while dressing the children can wait a few more minutes until the other explanatory rites are completed. A parent or godparent can hold the garment and place it on the child as the deacon says the accompanying text. The deacon does not need to place the garment on the children.

To begin the handing on of a lighted candle, the rite indicates that the deacon "takes the paschal candle and says: Receive the light of Christ."[61] Any deacon who has ever taken a lit paschal candle out of its stand knows how easily this can result in a shower of hot wax, especially if the paschal candle is large enough to be worthy of the symbolism of the light of Christ. If an assistant minister can carefully remove the paschal candle from its stand and either hold it or rest it on the floor, the deacon can place his hand on the candle as he says, "Receive the light of Christ." This also allows a parent or godparent of each child to light the baptismal candle from the paschal candle with ease. If removing the paschal candle from its stand is not possible, and if the paschal candle is quite tall, an assistant minister can use a small step stool to light the baptismal candles from the paschal candle or can light a taper in a long candle lighter from the paschal candle and then a parent or godparent of each child can light the baptismal candles from that taper. The deacon, placing his hand on the paschal candle, can say, "Receive the light of Christ," and then go on to say the rest of the accompanying text. It would be important to work out these details so that this part of the

60. OBC, 63.
61. OBC, 64.

rite flow smoothly and the details not obscure the symbolism of handing on the light of Christ.

The "ephphatha" derives its name from Jesus' cure of the man who was deaf and had a speech impediment: "Then looking up to heaven, he sighed and said to him, 'Ephphatha,' that is, 'Be opened.' And immediately his ears were opened, his tongue was released, and he spoke plainly."[62] The rite notes, "In the United States, the 'Ephphatha' Rite takes place at the discretion of the celebrant,"[63] so the deacon may decide whether to include it. The deacon says the accompanying text as he touches the ears and mouth of each child, although if there are many children, the deacon may just say the text without touching the ears and mouth of the children. If the "ephphatha" is used, the deacon should honor its beauty and meaning by clearly proclaiming the text and touching the ears and mouth of the children gracefully and with purpose. If there is an overriding concern about the length of time for a celebration of baptism with multiple children, it is preferable to omit the "ephphatha" or limit it to the text without any gesture, rather than rushing through it.

The transition from the celebration of baptism to the conclusion of the rite is marked by the third and final procession of the baptismal liturgy. If the baptism took place apart from the sanctuary in a place that was not visible to the assembly and if the whole assembly gathered there for the celebration of baptism, all join in this procession to the altar. If the baptism was celebrated in the sanctuary, the parents, godparents, children, and deacon make the short journey from the baptismal font to the altar. The rite indicates that "it is desirable that a baptismal canticle be sung"[64] during this procession, and several options for this canticle are provided. As with the two previous processions, the music for this procession is intended to accompany the action of processing and should not be prolonged when the procession ends.

Conclusion of the Rite

Standing in front of the altar, the deacon addresses the assembly and reminds them that the Christian initiation of the children, which has begun in baptism, will be completed in confirmation and the Eucharist.

---

62. Mark 7:34–35.
63. OBC, 65.
64. OBC, 67.

Then, he invites the assembly to join in praying the Lord's Prayer. The liturgy ends with a blessing of the parents and the rest of the assembly, a dismissal, and, "if circumstances suggest, a suitable canticle that expresses paschal joy and thanksgiving or the Canticle of the Blessed Virgin Mary, the Magnificat, [that] may be sung by all."[65] The rite provides four options for the blessing. The first three[66] are in the form of a solemn blessing, while the fourth[67] is a simpler prayer over the people.

Reflection Questions

1. Review the checklist in the appendix for a celebration of baptism outside of Mass. Are there people to assist you in this celebration so that you can focus on your role as the presider of the liturgy? If not, how might you go about recruiting and training people to serve as assistant ministers to help with the preparations and the details listed under "assistant minister responsibilities"?

2. What aspects of your role as presider and homilist in a celebration of baptism outside of Mass do you think need to be improved? Did this review of the rite suggest any changes that you might want to incorporate into your presiding or preaching?

---

65. OBC, 71.
66. OBC, 70, 247, 248.
67. OBC, 249.

PART 3

Nurturing Faith
in Families

Chapter 5

The Deacon's Role in Stimulating Faith

Parishes have developed a wide variety of ways to prepare parents for the baptism of their children. Some involve multiple sessions, while others take place during a single meeting. Some involve a visit to the parents' home, while others take place in the church or parish center. Some parishes encourage parents to do the preparation before the birth of the child, while others provide childcare and invite the parents to bring the child to the sessions. Some focus on catechesis on the meaning of baptism, while others employ faith-sharing conversations and suggestions for Christian parenting. Some provide an introduction to the baptismal liturgy, while others offer mystagogical reflections after the baptism. Some begin with a simple prayer, while others invite the parents into a more substantial opportunity for prayer during the session. Some parishes offer simple refreshments, while others build in time for the parents to socialize over a meal that the parish provides. Some use various written, audio-visual, and online resources from one or more Catholic publishers, while others do not.

While the model for the preparation of parents and the elements used in the preparation will vary from place to place, there are some overarching guiding principles. The *Code of Canon Law* states, "The parents of an infant to be baptized and those who are to undertake the function of sponsor are to be instructed properly on the meaning of this sacrament and the obligations attached to it. The pastor personally or through others is to take care that the parents are properly instructed through both pastoral advice and common prayer, bringing several families together and, where possible, visiting them."[1] The *Order of Baptism of Children* is primarily a liturgical book, but its two introductions address the preparation of parents who present their children for baptism and the faith formation of the children no fewer than ten times:

> The Church believes that there is nothing more ancient and nothing more proper for herself than to urge all—catechumens, parents of children who are to be baptized, and godparents—to that true and active faith by which, as they hold fast to Christ, they enter into or confirm the New Covenant. In fact, the pastoral instruction of catechumens and the preparation of parents, as well as the celebration of God's Word and the profession of baptismal faith, are all ordered to this end.[2]

> Preparation for Baptism and Christian instruction are of the highest concern for the People of God, that is, for the Church, which hands on and nourishes the faith received from the Apostles. Through the ministry of the Church, adults are called to the Gospel by the Holy Spirit and infants are baptized and brought up in her faith. Therefore, it is very important that, in the preparation for Baptism, catechists and other laypersons should work with Priests and Deacons.[3]

> It is the duty of pastors . . . with the assistance of catechists and other qualified laypersons, to prepare and assist the parents and godparents of children to be baptized through appropriate pastoral guidance.[4]

> Other Priests and Deacons, since they are co-workers in the ministry of Bishops and pastors, also prepare persons for Baptism.[5]

> To bring to completion the reality of the Sacrament, children should afterwards be formed in the faith in which they have been baptized. The foundation of this formation will be the Sacrament itself which they have already received. Christian formation, which by right is owed to the children, has no other purpose than to lead

---

1. CIC, c. 851.2.
2. CI, 3.
3. CI, 7.
4. CI, 13.
5. CI, 14.

them little by little to discern God's plan in Christ, so that ultimately they may be able to ratify the faith in which they have been baptized.[6]

Before the celebration of the Sacrament it is very helpful for the parents, either led by their own faith, or aided by the support of their friends or of other members of the community, to prepare themselves for an informed participation in the celebration by suitable means, such as books, articles, and catechisms aimed at the family. Furthermore, the pastor of the parish should take care to meet with them himself or through others, or even to bring together several families, to prepare them for the coming celebration by pastoral instructions and prayer in common.[7]

After the conferral of Baptism, the parents, grateful to God and faithful to the duty they have undertaken, are bound to guide their child to a knowledge of God, now his child by adoption. They are also bound to prepare the child to receive Confirmation and to participate in the Most Holy Eucharist. In this duty they are again to be helped in suitable ways by the pastor of the parish.[8]

It is for pastors to prepare families for the Baptism of their children and to help them fulfill the responsibility of formation, which they have now undertaken. Furthermore, it is for the Bishop to coordinate such pastoral initiatives in his diocese, with the help also of Deacons and laypeople.[9]

Since in many regions parents may not yet be ready for the celebration of Baptism, or they may ask that their children be baptized, even though they will not afterwards be brought up as Christians, and may even lose their faith, it is not sufficient that the parents be instructed in their faith and questioned about it in the rite itself. Conferences of Bishops, to help pastors of parishes, may issue pastoral directives, to determine a longer interval of time before the celebration of the Sacrament.[10]

---

6. OBC, 3.
7. OBC, 5.1.
8. OBC, 5.5.
9. OBC, 7.1.
10. OBC, 25.

During the meetings at which the parents are prepared for the Baptism of their children, it is of great importance that the instructions be supported by prayers and the rites. For this purpose it may help to use the various elements that are provided in the Order of Baptism for the celebration of the Word of God.[11]

Several themes emerge from these statements:

- The primary goal of the preparation of parents who present their children for baptism is to nurture their true and active faith.

- The preparation of parents should also lead to their informed participation in the celebration of baptism.

- Pastors, in collaboration with other priests, deacons, catechists, and laypersons, have a duty to prepare and assist the parents and godparents of children to be baptized.

- By presenting their children for baptism, parents accept the responsibility to raise their children in the faith.

- The postbaptismal formation of children completes the reality of the sacrament and leads them to receive Confirmation, participate in the Eucharist, and ratify their faith.

- The preparation of parents includes both instruction and prayer.

Many deacons, especially those in parish ministry, are involved in the preparation of parents who present their children for baptism. Deacons who are fathers bring particular experience to this ministry, a fact that is not lost on many pastors. In some places, the deacon is part of a baptismal ministry team along with catechists and other parishioners, while in other places, the deacon carries out this ministry alone. This ministry, while not unique to deacons, is particularly pertinent to deacons since their "principal function . . . is to collaborate with the bishop and the priests in the exercise of a ministry which is not of their own wisdom but of the Word of God, calling all to conversion and holiness."[12] Along with proclaiming the Gospel and preaching, the deacon serves the Church's ministry of the Word "as an evangelizer and teacher . . . [through] religious formation of candidates and families preparing for the reception of the sacraments."[13] Whether serving as part of a team

---

11. OBC, 27.
12. Congregation for the Clergy, *Directory for the Ministry and Life of Permanent Deacons*, 23.
13. United States Conference of Catholic Bishops, *National Directory for the Formation, Ministry, and Life of Permanent Deacons in the United States*, 31.

or undertaking this ministry alone, the deacon's role is that of evangelizer and teacher calling all to conversion and holiness.

The faith commitment of parents who present their children
for baptism varies greatly. Some are actively committed, some are
minimally committed or indifferent, and many are somewhere in
between. Wherever parents are in their faith development, the primary
goal of the deacon and other members of the baptismal ministry is to
help them grow in their faith. This involves both evangelization and
catechesis. Actively committed parents may benefit more from catechesis
that helps them to understand and practice their faith at a deeper level,
while minimally committed parents may benefit from a more basic
evangelization, "which will restore the joy of faith to their hearts and
inspire a commitment to the Gospel."[14] As evangelizer and teacher, the
deacon recognizes the complementary roles that evangelization (or first
proclamation) and catechesis play in the preparation of parents.
Catechesis, the *Directory for Catechesis*, 67, explains, develops the "inital
moment and brings it to maturity." Quoting from *Evangelii gaudium*,
the directory notes that catechesis and first proclamation are interwoven:

> "This first proclamation is called 'first' not because it exists at the
> beginning and can then be forgotten or replaced by other more
> important things. It is first in a qualitative sense because it is the
> principal proclamation, the one which we must hear again and
> again in different ways, the one which we must announce one way
> or another throughout the process of catechesis, at every level and
> moment." The first proclamation, the task of every Christian, is
> based on that "go" (Mark 16:15; Matthew 28:19) which Jesus gave
> as an instruction to his disciples and which implies going out,
> making haste, accompanying, thus becoming true missionary
> disciples. It therefore cannot be reduced to the conveying of a
> message, but is first of all sharing the life that comes from God
> and communicating the joy of having met the Lord.[15]

These three movements—go and welcome, proclaim and educate,
call and incorporate—provide an effective framework to approach
the preparation of parents.

---

14. EG, 14.
15. Pontifical Council for the Promotion of the New Evangelization, *Directory for Catechesis*, 61.

Evangelization implies reaching out to Catholic parents who may need an invitation to seek baptism for their children.

Go and Welcome

Effective evangelization and catechesis begin with hospitality. Just as the opening address of the baptismal liturgy echoes a spirit of welcome and joy,[16] so the initial interactions with parents by the deacon and other members of the baptismal ministry should manifest a spirit of welcome and joy. At a time when requesting baptism for one's child is increasingly countercultural, deacons and other pastoral ministers need to do everything they can to support the parents in their decision. Pope Francis made this clear when he said:

> In the mentality of the Gospel, you do not convince people with arguments, strategies or tactics. You convince them by simply learning how to welcome them. The Church is a mother with an open heart. She knows how to welcome and accept, especially

16. See OBC, 36.

those in need of greater care, those in greater difficulty.
The Church, as desired by Jesus, is the home of hospitality.[17]

Whether working as part of a baptismal ministry team or ministering on his own, the deacon should make sure that a sense of genuine welcome and hospitality characterizes all aspects of the preparation of parents, from the first contact the parents make with the parish to inquire about baptism to the healthy refreshments offered during preparation sessions for mothers who may be nursing.

Given the downward trend in the number of Catholic parents who request baptism for their children, the "go" part of this first movement cannot be overlooked. Evangelization implies not only responding to those parents who contact the parish to request baptism but also reaching out to Catholic parents who may need an invitation to seek baptism for their children. Pastors, deacons, and other pastoral ministers should remain attentive to news of Catholic parents who have recently welcomed a child into their families through birth or adoption. The deacon, another member of the pastoral staff, or a member of the baptismal ministry can proactively reach out to these parents with a card or phone call to congratulate the parents and to invite them to have their new child baptized. Even if this invitation is not accepted, the deacon or other person can assure the parents of the parish's prayers for them and their new child and can follow up with another invitation a few months later or on the child's first birthday.

Proclaim and Educate

The spirit of welcome and hospitality in the first movement provides an environment in which the second movement in the process can unfold: stimulating the faith of the parents. The *kerygma*, or basic message of the Gospel, is the foundation for this, whether the parents are actively or minimally committed to their faith. In *The Joy of the Gospel* (*Evangelii gaudium*), Pope Francis explains the necessity for conveying God's love:

> On the lips of the catechist the first proclamation must ring out over and over: "Jesus Christ loves you; he gave his life to save you; and now he is living at your side every day to enlighten,

---

17. Pope Francis, Homily at Asunción, Paraguay, July 12, 2015.

strengthen and free you." This first proclamation is called "first" not because it exists at the beginning and can then be forgotten or replaced by other more important things. It is first in a qualitative sense because it is the principal proclamation, the one which we must hear again and again in different ways, the one which we must announce one way or another throughout the process of catechesis, at every level and moment.[18]

While the impetus for parents participating is the coming baptism of their children, the reality is that the preparation is essentially "a discipleship session for adults who have kids preparing to celebrate Baptism."[19] Treating the parents as the adult learners that they are, the deacon and other members of the baptismal ministry can invite the parents to consider how they have experienced the presence of God and the love of Jesus Christ and how Jesus Christ has enlightened, strengthened, and freed them throughout the course of their lives. They can invite the parents to reflect on the meaning of baptism, on how they have responded to the call of their baptism, on how they have experienced dying and rising in their lives, and on how they want to fulfill their role as Christian parents. It is particularly helpful if a member of the baptismal ministry who is close in age and experience to the parents models this type of reflection by offering a brief witness from his or her experience, including any challenges encountered in acknowledging God among peers and in integrating faith in daily life.

The teaching component of the preparation can focus on the baptismal liturgy and its symbols both to prepare the parents for their informed participation in the coming celebration of baptism and to deepen their understanding and appreciation of the sacrament of baptism. The deacon and other members of the baptismal ministry can introduce the parents to some of the baptismal texts and symbols and invite them to consider how they reveal the meaning of baptism: for example, blessing of water, anointing with chrism, clothing with a white garment, handing on of a lighted candle.[20] During this part of the preparation, the parents can also be introduced to the questions that they will be asked at the beginning of the baptismal liturgy (what do you ask of God's Church

---

18. EG, 164.
19. Ken Ogorek, "Reaching Parents with the Gospel during Sacramental Prep," talk at FOCUS SLS conference, Phoenix, Arizona, December 31, 2019.
20. See, for example, chapter 2 above and Mary Ehle, *Baptized for Discipleship* (Chicago: LTP, 2019).

for your child, do you understand the responsibility you are undertaking to raise your child in the faith) and to the renunciation of sin and profession of faith that they will be invited to make prior to the baptism. The point is not simply to alert the parents to the answers to these questions but to invite them to ponder what answering these questions with authenticity and integrity will require of them on the day of the baptism and in the years ahead. Logistical details can be presented so that the parents know not only what to do on the day of the baptism but also the meaning behind these details: for example, bringing the child to the church in clothing other than the baptismal garment and then dressing the child in the baptismal garment after the baptism enfleshes the reality expressed in the text "You have become a new creation / and have clothed yourselves in Christ."[21]

Call and Incorporate

It is not unusual for parishes to lose contact with families in the years between the baptism and first Communion. Some parents are overwhelmed by the demands of parenting, some parents who both work Monday through Friday do not commit to Sunday Mass because they view the weekend strictly as leisure time, some parents have weekend jobs that interfere with attending Mass, some parents are fearful that their children won't behave in church, and some parents simply do not make raising their children in the practice of the faith a priority. At the same time, some parishes do not reach out and invite the parents of young children to get involved in the parish or to provide them with assistance in their role as Christian parents in the years after baptism. The preparation of parents prior to baptism is just one part of the Church's care for families and their faith formation. Just as the parents commit to raising their children in the faith after baptism, so the Church commits to assisting them in this process. Ideally, this does not mean just hoping that the parents and their children will return in about seven years for the child's first Communion. It means inviting parents and making efforts to incorporate them in parish life. The deacon and other members of the baptismal ministry should, at the very least, extend this invitation to parents at the end of the preparation session before baptism.

---

21. OBC, 63.

There are numerous possibilities for reaching out to young families that could be coordinated by the deacon, by other members of the baptismal ministry, or by a dedicated ministry to young families. This could include follow-up letters to the parents in the weeks and months after the baptism, a card on the anniversary of the child's baptism, and tips for effective Christian parenting as the child grows.[22] It could include monthly or even weekly gatherings in the parish center where parents with young children can socialize and get to know one another, where the children have a chance to play, and where the parents and children can participate in a faith-based activity. It could include faith-sharing and catechetical experiences for new parents, along with child-care to allow the parents to participate fully.[23] It should certainly include assurances that families with young children are always welcome at Mass, and ideally it should include a comfortable place where a parent can take a child who needs to be nursed or changed as well as a crying or restless child who needs a temporary change of venue. During the preparation sessions before baptism, parents could be asked which resources they would find most helpful.

Reflection Questions

1. What are the strengths of your current model for preparing parents who request baptism for their children? What are its limitations?

2. How might your current model for preparing parents be adapted or changed so that its primary focus is stimulating the faith of parents and forming them as disciples?

3. How might the texts and symbols of the baptismal liturgy be presented in parent preparation sessions to provide insight into the meaning of baptism?

4. How can you offer parents an opportunity to reflect prayerfully on the role that faith plays in their life during the preparation process?

5. What can you offer to parents after the baptism to help them grow in their faith and their role as Christian parents?

---

22. See, for example, Christopher Heller, *Infant Baptism Basics: A Parish Program* (Washington, DC: Pastoral Press, 1993) and *After the Plunge: Kit for Reaching Out to Parents after Baptism* (Alameda, CA: Pastoral Center, 2015).
23. See, for example, Ronald Rolheiser, *Longing for the Holy* (RENEW International), *Credible Catholic* (Magis Center) and *Discipleship Quads* (Steubenville Conferences).

Appendix

Questions and Answers

Are deacons considered ordinary ministers of baptism?

Yes, when the Second Vatican Council declared that the diaconate can be restored "as a proper and permanent rank of the hierarchy," it also declared that "it is a deacon's task, as authorized by the competent authority, to administer Baptism solemnly."[1] The *Code of Canon Law* states that "the ordinary minister of baptism is a bishop, a presbyter, or a deacon."[2] This is echoed in the *Order of Baptism of Children*, which states that "the ordinary ministers of Baptism are Bishops, Priests, and Deacons."[3]

When may a deacon baptize?

A deacon may baptize in a celebration of baptism outside of Mass at which he presides. In a celebration of baptism within Mass or a celebration of baptism outside of Mass at which a bishop or priest presides, the bishop or priest who presides would normally baptize. When many children are baptized in such a celebration, however, a deacon may assist the bishop or priest by baptizing some of the children.[4] A deacon may baptize a child in danger of death using the shorter rite of baptism in chapter 5 of the *Order of Baptism of Children*.[5]

---

1. LG, 29.
2. CIC, c. 861.1.
3. CI, 11.
4. CI, 15; OBC, 61, 124, 256, 286.
5. OBC, 22.

May a deacon baptize a child during the Easter Vigil?

The rubrics for the Easter Vigil in *The Roman Missal* indicate that "the Priest baptizes the adult elect and the children."[6] When the *Order of Baptism of Children* addresses the baptism of children during the Easter Vigil, however, it refers to the section in the rite that states, "If there are many children to be baptized, and there are several Priests or Deacons present, each of them may baptize some of the children."[7] It would seem, then, that a deacon may assist the priest by baptizing some of the children when multiple children are baptized during the Easter Vigil.

May a deacon baptize in a church where he is not assigned for ministry?

The *Code of Canon Law* states that, "except in a case of necessity, no one is permitted to confer baptism in the territory of another without the required permission, not even upon his own subjects."[8] A deacon who wishes to baptize in a church where he is not assigned for ministry needs to request and receive permission from the pastor of that church. If the church is outside of the deacon's diocese, he will usually be required to submit a letter of good standing from his bishop.

Why does the Church desire that baptisms occur on Sunday?

As the *Code of Canon Law* notes, "Although Baptism can be celebrated on any day, it is nevertheless recommended that it be celebrated on Sunday or, if possible, at the Easter Vigil."[9] The reason is related to the meaning of baptism: "Those who are baptized are united with Christ in a death like his, are buried with him in death, and also in him are given life and are raised up. For in Baptism nothing other than the Paschal Mystery is recalled and accomplished, because in it human beings pass from the death of sin into life."[10] Since the Easter Vigil and Sunday are the days when the Church commemorates the Lord's resurrection, they

---

6. RM, The Easter Vigil in the Holy Night, 50.
7. OBC, 28.2, 61.
8. CIC, c. 862.
9. CIC, c. 856.
10. CI, 6.

are considered the optimum days for celebrating baptism, which incorporates people into Christ's death and resurrection.

Why would one use the option to baptize by immersion?

While baptism may be celebrated by immersion or by pouring water over the child's head, liturgical documents consistently state a preference for immersion because it "more suitably signifies participation in the Death and Resurrection of Christ."[11] As a sacramental people, Catholics experience and come to understand their faith through signs and symbols, as well as through words, so using the most effective signs and symbols is important. In immersion, a person goes down into the water and then comes up out of the water, just as Christ went into the tomb and then rose. Pouring water over a child's head, while meeting the requirement for a valid baptism, does not convey this symbolism nearly as well.

Doesn't baptizing multiple children in the same celebration take a lot of time?

With proper preparation, the Church's preference for "a common celebration of Baptism on the same day for all newborn babies"[12] does not necessarily result in unduly long celebrations of baptism. In a celebration of baptism outside of Mass with a deacon presiding, one or more assistant ministers can attend to details that the presider does not need to do by himself and that would take extra time if he did them by himself. (See the "assistant minister responsibilities" in the "Checklist for the *Order of Baptism of Children*.") The rite also notes that there are elements that can be omitted or combined when a large number of children are baptized. The questions during the rite of receiving the children may be addressed to all the parents at once, and the parents may respond to the second and third questions together.[13] In the Liturgy of the Word, a single Scripture may be read and the homily should be brief.[14] The anointing before baptism and the "ephphatha" rite may be omitted.[15]

---

11. CI, 22.
12. CI, 27.
13. OBC, 38–39.
14. OBC, 44–45.
15. OBC, 51, 65.

Should a deacon direct the parish's prebaptismal preparation for parents?

Since a deacon is called to serve as an evangelizer and teacher and to assist the pastor with the religious formation of families who are preparing for the celebration of sacraments, it is appropriate for him to be involved in prebaptismal preparation for parents. The pastor may determine that he is best qualified to direct this ministry, but the pastor may also determine that another member of the pastoral staff or a parishioner is better qualified to be the director or that the deacon needs to devote his time to other ministries. In some places, a deacon may serve in this ministry alone, while in other places he may be part of a team of people who collaborate in this ministry.

How can a deacon effectively minister to parents and preside at celebrations of baptism in a multicultural community?

Like any pastoral minister, the deacon needs to recognize that he is part of a particular ethnicity and culture and that his ethnicity and culture are not necessarily normative, especially in multicultural communities. When ministering with and to people from other ethnicities and cultures, the deacon needs to be humble, seeking to accompany them and learn from them. He should consider himself as at the service of all people in the parish, for each culture "offers positive values and forms which can enrich the way the Gospel is preached, understood and lived."[16] Although likely inspired by good intentions, an approach that suggests that the deacon is colorblind or sees beyond ethnic and cultural differences often does more harm than good. "Jesus came to restore us, redeem us, and release us for his kingdom mission, not in spite of our ethnicities, but in our ethnic identities. For example, if you are a white man or woman hoping to share Jesus with a black community, you need to know their context and your context in order to be able to share the gospel in a transformative way. Sharing the gospel is never about being safe or polite. It's about loving deeply, and you can't love what you do not know."[17] The deacon can recruit and train parishioners from the various

---

16. Pope John Paul II, *Ecclesia in Oceania*, 16.
17. Sarah Shin, *Beyond Colorblind: Redeeming Our Ethnic Journey* (Downers Grove, IL: InterVarsity Press, 2017), 22.

ethnicities and cultures in the parish to serve on the baptismal ministry team and to assist with baptismal liturgies. He can learn enough of a different language to preside at the celebration of baptism outside of Mass with people who speak that language as their primary or only language. He can speak with priests, deacons, and other people who are from a particular ethnicity or culture to understand customs related to baptism, such as the role of godparents who, in some Latino communities, Bishop Ricardo Ramírez explains, "dress the child in his or her baptismal clothes, or are responsible for purchasing the baptismal outfit. Baptism in New Mexico is followed by a home ritual in which the godparents present the newly baptized child to his or her parents. As they do so, they say, 'Compadre y comadre: les entregamos esta rosa que salió con los santos sacramentos y el agua que recibió; se llama _____. (Compadre and comadre, we give you this rose that came from the Holy Sacraments and from the water received; his/her name is _____.)"[18]

---

18. Bishop Ricardo Ramírez, *Power from the Margins: The Emergence of the Latino in the Church and in Society* (Maryknoll, NY: Orbis Books, 2016), 115.

Checklist for the *Order of Baptism of Children*

I. Celebration of Baptism within Sunday Mass with a Deacon Assisting

Remote Preparations:

❑ Let the scheduled greeters, servers, readers, and music ministers know that baptism will be celebrated at this Mass.

❑ Alert the reader if a reading from the "Conferral of Infant Baptism" section of the *Lectionary for Mass* will replace one of the readings of the day.

❑ Decide who will do each of the things on the "assistant minister responsibilities" list.

❑ Include one or more intercessions related to the baptism in the prayer of the faithful.

❑ Speak with the music minister about music for the following:

    ❑ Procession from church door to altar: _____

    ❑ Litany of the Saints: _____

    ❑ Procession to baptistery: _____

    ❑ Acclamation after baptism: _____

❑ Ask the parents to do the following:

    ❑ Arrive at the church fifteen to thirty minutes before the time of the Mass.

❑ Dress the child to be baptized in clothes other than the baptismal garment.

❑ Bring the baptismal garment to the church.

❑ Line up a relative or friend who can take the child to be baptized and other small children to another location during the Liturgy of the Word, if necessary.

❑ Make sure there are enough clean bath towels for the number of children who will be baptized by immersion.

❑ Announce the baptism in the parish bulletin and social media, and invite parishioners to participate in the baptismal liturgy.

❑ Prepare a clean and comfortable place where the children can be nursed before the liturgy if necessary, where the children can be taken during the Liturgy of the Word, where the children's diapers can be changed, and where the parents can dress the children in the baptismal garments following the baptism. If possible, set up a television or other monitor so that those in this space can see and hear what is occurring in the church.

Immediate Preparations:

❑ If the baptismal font is not heated, add warm water to the font.

❑ Light the paschal candle.

❑ Set out the following in the baptistery:

  ❑ Oil of catechumens

  ❑ Sacred chrism

  ❑ Small towel for wiping the presider's hands after the anointings

  ❑ Bath towel for each child if baptizing by immersion

  ❑ Baptismal candle for each child

❑ Set the ribbons in the *Order of Baptism of Children* to the pages needed during the liturgy.

❑ Set the ribbons in the *Lectionary for Mass* to the selected readings.

❑ Set out a copy of the prayer of the faithful for the presider and the deacon or reader.

Assistant Minister Responsibilities:

- Greet the families and friends of the children to be baptized as they arrive at the church, show them to their seats, and point out the location of restrooms and, if needed, the place where the children can be nursed and where diapers can be changed.

- Accompany the parents, godparents, and children to be baptized to the door of the church a few minutes before Mass begins.

- Hold a microphone for the parents so that their responses at the door of the church can be heard by all in the assembly.

- Accompany the parents, godparents, and children in the procession from the door of the church to their seats in the church.

- Accompany those who take the children for the Liturgy of the Word to the separate place prepared for them.

- Accompany those who took the children for the Liturgy of the Word from the separate place back into the church prior to the litany of saints.

- Remind the parents to loosen the children's clothing during the litany of saints so that the priest can anoint the children on the breast with the oil of catechumens (unless this anointing is omitted).

- Hand the container with the oil of catechumens to the priest for the anointing before baptism (unless this anointing is omitted).

- Take the container with the oil of catechumens from the priest after the anointing before baptism (unless this anointing is omitted).

- Give the priest a hand towel to wipe his hands after the anointing before baptism (unless this anointing is omitted).

- Accompany the parents, godparents, and children to be baptized to the baptistery or other place where baptism will be celebrated. Remind the parents or godparents to bring the white baptismal garment with them.

- For baptism by immersion, hand each set of parents a bath towel in which to wrap their child after the baptism.

- Direct the parents, godparents, and children to the place where they will stand for the anointing after baptism and other explanatory rites.

- Hand the container with the sacred chrism to the priest for the anointing after baptism.

- Take the container with the sacred chrism from the priest after the anointing after baptism.

- Give the priest a hand towel to wipe his hands after the anointing after baptism.
- Give a baptismal candle to a parent or godparent of each child for the handing on of a lighted candle.
- If the flame of the paschal candle is too high to reach:
  - take the paschal candle out of its stand and hold the paschal candle so that a parent or godparent of each child can light the child's baptismal candle, or
  - light a taper in a long candle lighter from the paschal candle, and hold this taper so that a parent or godparent of each child can light the child's baptismal candle, or
  - using a small step stool, light each baptismal candle from the paschal candle, and hand a lit baptismal candle to a parent or godparent of each child.
- Direct the parents, godparents, and children back to their seats or to a place where they can dress the children in the white baptismal garments after the "ephphatha" (or after the handing on of a lighted candle if the ephphatha is omitted).

II. Celebration of Baptism outside of Mass with a Deacon Presiding

Remote Preparations:

❏ Schedule liturgical ministers:

  ❏ Greeter(s): _____

  ❏ Server/Assistant Minister: _____

  ❏ Reader: _____

  ❏ Music Minister(s): _____

❏ Choose the Scripture reading(s): _____

❏ Prepare the prayer of the faithful.

❏ Let the reader know which reading(s) to prepare, and send the reader a copy of the prayer of the faithful.

❏ Decide who will do each task on the "assistant minister responsibilities" list.

❏ Discuss the music that the music minister will use:

   ❏ Opening psalm or hymn: _____

   ❏ Procession from church door to lectern: _____

   ❏ Responsorial psalm: _____

   ❏ Litany of the saints: _____

   ❏ Procession from lectern to baptistery: _____

   ❏ Acclamation after baptism: _____

   ❏ Procession from baptistery to altar: _____

   ❏ Canticle after blessing and dismissal: _____

❏ Ask the parents to do the following:

   ❏ Arrive at the church fifteen to thirty minutes before the time of the baptism.

   ❏ Dress the child to be baptized in clothes other than the baptismal garment.

   ❏ Bring the baptismal garment to the church.

   ❏ Line up a relative or friend who can take the child to be baptized and other small children to another location during the Liturgy of the Word, if necessary.

❏ Announce the baptism in the parish bulletin and social media, and invite parishioners to participate in the baptismal liturgy.

❏ Prepare a clean and comfortable place where the children can be nursed before the liturgy if necessary, where the children can be taken during the Liturgy of the Word, where the children's diapers can be changed, and where the parents can dress the children in the baptismal garments following the baptism. If possible, set up a television or other monitor so that those in this space can see and hear what is occurring in the church.

Immediate Preparations:

❏ If the baptismal font is not heated, add warm water to the font.

❏ Light the paschal candle.

❏ Set out the following in the baptistery:

    ❏ Oil of catechumens

    ❏ Sacred chrism

    ❏ Small towel for wiping the presider's hands after the anointings

    ❏ Bath towel for each child if baptizing by immersion

    ❏ Baptismal candle for each child

❏ Set the ribbons in the *Order of Baptism of Children* to the pages needed during the liturgy.

❏ Set the ribbons in the *Lectionary for Mass* to the selected reading(s).

❏ Set out a copy of the prayer of the faithful for the presider and the reader.

Assistant Minister Responsibilities:

- Greet the families and friends of the children to be baptized as they arrive at the church, show them to their seats, and point out the location of restrooms and, if needed, the place where the children can be nursed and where diapers can be changed.

- Accompany the parents, godparents, and children to be baptized to the door of the church a few minutes before the liturgy begins.

- Hold a microphone for the parents so that all in the assembly can hear their responses at the door of the church.

- Accompany the parents, godparents, and children in the procession from the door of the church to their seats in the church.

- Accompany those who take the children for the Liturgy of the Word to the separate place prepared for them.

- Accompany those who took the children for the Liturgy of the Word from the separate place back into the church prior to the litany of saints.

- Remind the parents to loosen the children's clothing during the litany of saints so that the deacon can anoint the children on the breast with the oil of catechumens (unless this anointing is omitted).

- Hand the container with the oil of catechumens to the deacon for the anointing before baptism (unless this anointing is omitted).

- Take the container with the oil of catechumens from the deacon after the anointing before baptism (unless this anointing is omitted).

- Give the deacon a hand towel to wipe his hands after the anointing before baptism (unless this anointing is omitted).

- Accompany the parents, godparents, and children to be baptized to the baptistery or other place where baptism will be celebrated. Remind the parents or godparents to bring the white baptismal garment with them.

- For baptism by immersion, hand each set of parents a bath towel in which to wrap their child after the baptism.

- Direct the parents, godparents, and children to the place where they will stand for the anointing after baptism and other explanatory rites.

- Hand the container with the chrism to the deacon for the anointing after baptism.

- Take the container with the chrism from the deacon after the anointing after baptism.

- Give the deacon a hand towel to wipe his hands after the anointing after baptism.

- Give a baptismal candle to a parent or godparent of each child for the handing on of a lighted candle.

- If the flame of the paschal candle is too high to reach:
  - take the paschal candle out of its stand and hold the paschal candle so that a parent or godparent of each child can light the child's baptismal candle, or
  - light a taper in a long candle lighter from the paschal candle, and hold this taper so that a parent or godparent of each child can light the child's baptismal candle, or
  - using a small step stool, light each baptismal candle from the paschal candle, and hand a lit baptismal candle to a parent or godparent of each child.

- Direct the parents, godparents, and children back to their seats or to a place where they can dress the children in the white baptismal garments after the ephphatha (or after the handing on of a lighted candle if the ephphatha is omitted).

- Accompany the parents, godparents, and children to the altar for the concluding rites.